FAITH INTO ABUNDANCE

Ainsley & Allen Publishing

NEWARK, DELAWARE

Ainsley & Allen Publishing LLC
2035 Sunset Lake Road
Newark, DE 19702
www.ainsleyallenpublishing.com

Ordering Information:
Quantity sales. Special discounts are available on quantity purchases by corporations, associations, and others. For details, contact the "Special Sales Department" at the address above.

Faith Into Abundance. —1st ed.
978-0-9975855-1-3

Library of Congress Control Number: 2016955361

ARE YOU A CHRISTIAN ENTREPRENEUR?

Due to the popularity of this book, the publisher has approved a second volume and we are looking for people with inspiring stories of faith that lead into abundance.

To learn how you can be part of the next volume of *FAITH INTO ABUNDANCE,* visit http://AinsleyAllenPublishing.com/apply-faith/

In addition to being a powerful way to give back to the entrepreneurial community, it will be great exposure for you and your company.

Ainsley & Allen Publishing is donating all royalties from the retail sales of *FAITH INTO ABUNDANCE* to SOLID ROCK INTERNATIONAL, a Christian non-profit 501(c)3 organization focused on transforming the body, mind, and soul of the poor in the Dominican Republic.

> *"Anyone who listens to my teaching and follows it is wise, like a person who builds a house on solid rock. Though the rain comes and the floodwaters rise and the winds beat against the house, it won't collapse because it is built on bedrock." –Matthew 7:24-25*

You can learn more about Solid Rock International by visiting SolidRockInternational.org

AUTHORS

Brian Ainsley Horn

Carmen Sakurai

Robert Thornton

Jillian Quinn

Mike "Mountainman" Lamborne

David Norrie

Scott Jones And Brian Krider

Lisa Avedon

Stephen F. Skinner

Jaime Smith

Cydney Bulger, Esq.

Jim Schneider

Demitrus Evans

Malcolm X. Adams

Lisa Ashe

David D. Simons

Jennifer Xue

Gary LeBlanc

Dan Vallee

Brant Phillips

Patsy Rae Dawson

Dr. Ron Eccles

Matt LaClear

Ashley Hill

John Rowley

Phillip Singleton

Ben Malick

Zondra Wilson

Don Schnure

Howard Partridge

Mayra Fernandez

Lory Moore

CONTENTS

INTRODUCTION

When Christians hear the expression "glorifying God," they probably think of worship, evangelism, giving, and faith. I think most Christians in business already understand how business can contribute to those four ways of glorifying God.

However, many do not understand is that there is a fifth way to glorify Him as an entrepreneur – one that we often overlook, but one that has profound implications for any believer that owns a business. This fifth way to glorify God is imitation – imitation of the attributes of God – and it is critical to understand how business in itself glorifies God.

God created us so that we would imitate him and so that he could look at us and see something of his wonderful attributes reflected in us. To be in God's image means to be like God and to represent God on the earth. If you are a parent, you know that there is a special joy that comes when you see your children imitating some of your good qualities and following some of the moral standards that you have tried to model.

With this background, we can now turn to consider specific aspects of business activity and ask how they provide unique opportunities for glorifying God through imitation. We will find that in every aspect of business there are multiple layers of opportunities to give glory to God.

We know that producing goods from the earth is fundamentally good in itself because it is part of the purpose for which God put us on the earth. Imagine what would happen if we were able somehow to transport Adam and Eve into a twenty-first century American home.

After we gave them appropriate clothing, we would turn on the faucet to offer them a glass of water, and they would ask, "What's that?" When we explained that the pipes enabled us to have water whenever we wanted it, they would exclaim, "Do you mean to say that God has put in the earth materials that would enable you to make that water system?"

"Yes," we would reply.

"Then praise God for giving us such a great earth! And praise him for giving us the knowledge and skill to be able to make that water system!"

The refrigerator would elicit even more praise to God from their lips. And so would the electric lights and the newspaper and the oven and the telephone, and so forth. Their hearts would brim over with thankfulness to the Creator who had hidden such wonderful materials in the earth and had also given to human beings such skill in working with them.

Therefore, in contrast to some economic theories, productive work is not evil or undesirable in itself, or something to be avoided, nor does the Bible ever view positively the idea of retiring early and not working at anything again. Rather, work in itself is also something that is fundamentally good and God-given.

What about having employees?

In contrast to Marxist theory, the Bible does not view it as evil for one person to hire another person and to gain profit from that person's work. It is not necessarily "exploiting" the employee. Rather, Jesus said, "the laborer deserves his wages" (Luke 10:7), implicitly approving the idea of paying wages to employees. In fact, Jesus' parables often speak of servants and masters, and of people paying others for their work, with no hint that hiring people to work for wages is evil or wrong.

This is a wonderful ability that God has given us. Paying another person for his or her labor is an activity that is uniquely human. It is shared by no other creature. The ability to work for other people for pay, or to pay other people for their work, is another way that God has created us so that we would be able to glorify him more fully in such relationships. When the employment arrangement is working properly, both parties benefit.

What about buying and selling?

Several passages of Scripture assume that buying and selling are morally right. In fact, buying and selling are necessary for anything beyond subsistence level living, and these activities are another part of what distinguishes us from the animal kingdom. No individual or family providing for all its needs could produce more than a very low standard of living (that is if it could buy and sell absolutely nothing and had to live off only what it could produce itself, which would be a fairly simple range of foods and clothing). But when we can sell what we make and buy from others who specialize in producing milk or bread, orange juice or blueberries, bicycles or televisions, cars or computers, then, through the mechanism of buying and selling, we can all obtain a much higher standard of living, and thereby we fulfill God's purpose that we enjoy the resources of the earth.

What about earning a profit?

Some people will object that earning a profit is "exploiting" other people. It might be if there is a great disparity in power or knowledge between you and me and I cheat you or charge an exorbitant price when you have nowhere else to go and you need food or water.

If profit is made in a system of voluntary exchange, then when I earn a profit I also help you. You are better off because you have a pair of shoes that you wanted, and I am better off because I earned $4 profit, and that keeps me in business and makes me want to make more shoes to sell. Everybody wins, and nobody is exploited. Through this process, I glorify God by enlarging the possessions over which I can exercise wise stewardship.

The ability to earn a profit is thus the ability to multiply our resources while helping other people. It is a wonderful ability that God gave us, and it is not evil or morally neutral but fundamentally good. Through the inspiring stories in this book, you'll see how entrepreneurs have glorified God through their business, and changed lives.

HOW TO USE THIS BOOK

Read one chapter per day. You may be tempted to do a little "binge reading," but resist the temptation. Stick to one per day and bookmark the pages or phrases that resonate with you. You will want to refer to your bookmarked items when you are facing challenges and doubt. I recommend you even make notes on a sheet of paper as you work through the book.

Each of these stories is from a different Christian entrepreneur and has a lesson that will be uniquely beneficial to anyone who reads it. What one person learns from one story could be totally different than what another person learns from the same story. As you go through the book, you will start to see a pattern in your notes. This can provide a template to help you fall back on faith in God more.

Share this book with family, friends, your Sunday school class, and Bible study members. Give a copy to a local business owner that needs a boost. When you need a reminder that God has great plans for you, or that He can turn a temporary setback to life changing abundance, return to this book again.

If you are a Christian entrepreneur and would like to be considered for our next book, please send an email to me at brian@authorityalchemy.com.

I hope you enjoy the book!

Brian Ainsley Horn

THE DAY I LOST MY SON

BRIAN AINSLEY HORN

> *"So do not fear, for I am with you; do not be dismayed, for I am your God. I will strengthen you and help you; I will uphold you with my righteous right hand."*
>
> *Isaiah 41:10*

No matter how far I have come in my life and my career, the birth of my son was by far the happiest day of my life. Jackson was born on a Monday in the Spring of 2010. While we were waiting to go home on Tuesday, the nurse came in to do final checks on Mom and Jackson.

While she was checking Jackson, she noted that his temperature was a little cold. So, she took him to the nurse's station to run further checks on him. But she insisted that it was no big deal. Less than 10 minutes later my mother-in-law came running into the room. She had tears running down her face.

She said, "Something's wrong with Jackson. Something's wrong with Jackson. Come quick."

I started running down the hall and over the intercom I heard, "Code Blue. Code Blue. Code Blue." A doctor and nurses were blowing past us at full speed.

Once we got there, we saw our poor little six-pound baby completely blue in color. He wasn't moving.

The doctors and nurses started to work on him and get him breathing again. Thankfully, in just ten seconds (but felt like hours) his color started to come back and he began to breathe.

After a few moments, the doctor came out and said that they were going to have to put him in the NICU (Neonatal Intensive Care Unit).

They took him away from us and rushed him to the NICU. We had to wait about an hour before we were able to see him again - and when I did see him, my heart broke.

He had a breathing tube and all types of different monitoring devices on his chest. He was totally covered in wires.

He also had a huge needle sticking in the top of his head. and a shaved patch of hair. You see, a baby's vein is too small for an IV in their arm, so they have to put the IV in their head. So, they shaved a patch at the top of Jackson's head for it. They had to stick his head with needles three times before they could get a proper vein.

After a while, the doctor pulled us aside and said, "We don't know what's wrong with him. We're going to have to do tests."

He went on to the most horrible sounding things that you could imagine. Every single one was worse than the next. I lived at the NICU for the next several days. The doctors came back every day, and let us know what conditions they were able to rule out.

It started to look like what happened was "just something that happened" and probably nothing to worry about. Everything was going to be okay.

The nurses told us that he was doing very well. He was eating on his own and was off the breathing tube. It looked like we were going to take him home.

We walked into the NICU on a Thursday morning, just hours before Jackson was going to be discharged. The doctor was there and asked us to sit down.

The doctor said, "I'm sorry to inform you, but your son has Down syndrome."

It was like the world stopped. I never thought in a million years that would be something I would deal with. Everything was in slow motion.

Then the doctor proceeded to list all the things that Jackson was not going to be able to do. The first thing he said was that he wasn't going to be able to crawl like a typical child. He would be much older before that happened. He also said that he would not walk until he was much older. Jackson would probably not recognize us as his parents for a while. We would also have to take care of him for the rest of our lives. But if we were lucky, he could have a job sacking groceries one day.

It was crushing. At that moment it was like my son had died.

The little boy I'd dreamed my whole life about was gone, and I had this new child. I was still excited about him and still loved him, but everything the doctor was telling us was awful.

I was angry at God. I thought this was punishment for all my past sins and mistakes. My faith was gone.

As his health continued to improve, we brought him home with us early the next week. He was doing extremely well...eating great, sleeping 6 hours at a stretch, etc.

Even though everything was going perfect, I couldn't get what the doctor told us out of my head. I kept thinking about what he wouldn't be able to do, especially the crawling.

Playing on the floor with my son crawling to me was a mental image I carried with me for as long as I can remember. That seemed to be tainted now.

Well, a couple of nights after we brought him home, I was lying in bed watching TV with Jackson on my stomach. Suddenly, he started to kick and push with his little legs. So I put my hand by his feet and he pushed off of them.

He slid up. I put them a little higher, and he slid up. Within 20-30 seconds he had moved all the way up to my neck.

I was crying like a baby.

Jackson "crawled."

The first thing the doctor said he wouldn't be able to do, he did within two weeks. God spoke directly to me that night.

THE LESSON OF FAITH

Jackson didn't listen to the doctor; I did. I listened to every single word he said. But Jackson believed that he could do things. That was a powerful life lesson I learned from that little two-week-old baby.

That simple act of him crawling up my chest renewed my faith.

When I felt like giving up, I was missing out on what God has to offer. Know that you are not alone, and know that we are in the hands of God. He will provide us with strength when we need it.... just like Jackson had that strength to crawl up my body.

INTO ABUNDANCE

At that point, I wiped out everything that the doctor said he wouldn't be able to do. I didn't believe a word of it anymore.

I was a successful SEO consultant at the time. But, I had an idea to create a platform that would build backlinks to customers' websites. This was an important factor to rank sites in Google at the time. It would be automated and allow me to go from a handful of clients to hundreds without needing to add much staff.

Everyone - from my bigger clients, to other SEO consultants - all told me not to do it. They said that I had it made as a consultant to some the biggest names in the information marketing world. They said I was crazy for trying something so risky as developing a SaS.

I had pretty much written off the idea. But, Jackson didn't listen to the experts. So, I decided not to listen either.

Within 8 months, it became a near six-figure a month business.

APPLICATION

Pray and meditate on something you've written off as impossible. If you can't remember one, pray and meditate on that.

You are reading this book, this chapter, and this sentence for a reason.

There is something that an "expert" has convinced you is impossible. But it's not impossible through God.

There is no limit and you can do anything God puts on your heart.

PRAYER

God, I come before you today to thank You for this lesson in faith. Help me to trust that you have a special plan for my life. Please Lord, bless me with abundance so that I may honor You with good works by supporting my community. I trust You in all things.

DAILY DECLARATION

Everything and everyone is put in our path for a purpose. We just have to pay attention to discover God's reason. #FaithIntoAbundance

MEET BRIAN HORN

Best-selling author and entrepreneur, Brian Ainsley Horn, helps professionals leverage their knowledge to gain authority status in their industry, then uses "authority marketing" to get them national media exposure.

His unique method has been talked about and covered on The Howard Stern Show, Wall Street Journal, ABC, Perez Hilton, CBS News, Forbes, Advertising Age and dozens of other media outlets.

Inc Magazine named Brian an "emerging business leader to watch."

Brian is a regular contributor to Entrepreneur Magazine, Huffington Post and The Examiner.

He is an in-demand speaker that has traveled the world entertaining and educating audiences.

Brian is also a proud father, Nak Muay and an advocate for children with Down syndrome.

CONTACT BRIAN

WEBSITE
AuthorityAlchemy.com

FACEBOOK
Facebook.com/Brian.Horn

EMAIL
brian@authorityalchemy.com

TWITTER
@brianhorn

LINKEDIN
LinkedIn.com/in/BrianAinsleyHorn

DAY 2

WHEN GOD FORGOT ABOUT ME

CARMEN SAKURAI

> *"For I know the plans that I have for you,' declares the LORD, 'plans for welfare and not for calamity to give you a future and a hope." -*
>
> *Jeremiah 29:11*

"I never loved you. I'm not ready to be a dad. Come to think of it, I hated you before I even met you. You make me want to kill myself."

They sound like cruel words coming from an angry, irresponsible teenage boy discovering his girlfriend is pregnant. But they're not. They were spoken to me on Oct 2, 2006, by the man I have been with for 15 years, married for 11; and with whom I share a beautiful five-year old son - Joshua Gabriel.

Rewind one month. It was a chilly September morning. The three of us had tears in our eyes as we stood in the airport saying our goodbyes. Joshua and I were relocating to Las Vegas while my husband remained in Chicago to prepare for his job transfer to Las Vegas the following March. We agreed that J and I would fly out ahead so the little Kindergartener could settle into his new school since the year had just begun. "Take good care of your mommy ok, buddy?" were the words we heard as the two of us walked to the gate.

"God... please give us strength and keep us all safe. Please bring him to us quickly so we can be a happy family again!"

Two long weeks later, my husband flew in to visit us. J and I were ecstatic! The morning after he arrived, we chatted about his move, and I asked my husband for reassurance that everything will be ok. He turned to me with the coldest, emptiest eyes I've ever seen and said, "I never loved you. I'm not ready to be a dad. Come to think of it, I hated you before I even met you. You make me want to kill myself. I never wanted to marry you. You don't have what it takes to be a good wife or a good mother. I don't want to be happy as a family... I want to find my own happiness. I'm tired of pretending. I want a divorce."

I felt as though liquids of pure, excruciating pain shot through my veins and into my heart... I couldn't breathe. What did I do wrong? What happened while we were apart? I wanted to be dead. Surely not being alive must feel less painful than THIS. My mind was filled with panic and confusion; I was unable to register any of this properly. He has been my best friend, partner, and the head of our little family for almost half of my life. We had plans for a big family... a dozen kids we would raise to become exceptional people and leave a powerful legacy. My purpose was to love, adore, and take care of my husband, our son, and all our future children.

But within minutes, the only world I knew was completely shattered without warning. I didn't know what to do... how was I supposed to live without him? How was I supposed to raise my baby alone? He gathered his things, and within an hour, he threw away our 15 years together and removed himself from our lives.

I had been abandoned... left to raise a little boy alone... far, far away from everything and everyone I knew. I was so scared my baby and I would not survive.

The following month, I discovered he had been having an affair and needed to "get rid" of what's been holding him back... me and my baby. There were no plans of a job transfer. I had absolutely no idea. I felt betrayed. But even more, I felt like a horrible, ugly, worthless failure.

God had completely forgotten about me.

THE LESSON OF FAITH

I was still trying to get myself back on my feet, but the noise from others was so distracting, I would repeatedly fall right back down in defeat. "What do you think you did to make him cheat on you?" "He probably got bored of you." "What a shame... every boy needs a dad." "Maybe if you lost some weight..." "You could probably gain some weight..." "You need to stop being so needy." "You need to stop being so independent." I just couldn't win. I didn't understand any of this. I've always been a devout Catholic... a religious education teacher. I was so angry at God... What exactly am I being punished for?

"God... remember me? I'm very sorry for whatever wrong I'm being punished for. Please fix this. Please bring him back to his senses so we can be a family again!"

Then one evening, as I was holding my son before he went to sleep, I began to cry... "I love you so much, Joshua. I promise to do my very best to fix our family, and we'll be ok just like before... so please hang in there." My five year old looked at me with his big, sweet eyes and said, "Mommy, this IS our family... you and me. THIS is our new life. You're doing perfect! Please don't waste your tears on someone who can't see how special we are. God chose you as my guardian angel and I love you and I trust you with my life... so please trust God the way I trust you."

If I'm his guardian angel, then this round-eyed five-year-old is my precious messenger sent from God. He is Joshua Gabriel... named after Angel Gabriel after all.

Blessed with those words of pure love and trust, I HAD TO BELIEVE God loves me just as much as He loves the happiest and most successful people... I HAD TO BELIEVE He wouldn't have gifted me this incredible little boy if He didn't trust my strength, intelligence, and my capacity to love. I HAD TO BELIEVE there was a REAL PURPOSE to why I've been challenged to find a way to overcome and recover from this most awful experience and its effects on me. I HAD TO FORGIVE EVERYONE who hurt me... and I had to learn to see myself through God's eyes.

"God... please strengthen my faith in your plans for me and my baby. Please open my eyes so that I may see the goodness that YOU see. May YOUR will be done."

INTO ABUNDANCE

God has promised us an ABUNDANCE of WINS, but only if we FOLLOW THROUGH no matter what blocks our path; including the most painful and difficult of events in our lives. The faithful always win because the One who created the highest mountains, the deepest seas, the entire universe and beyond... is on our side. I was ready to do whatever it took for my win.

I set my mind to trust in God as my child confidently trusted in me. I let go of the "idea" of my happy family. I let go of needing to prove and explain myself to anyone and everyone with an opinion about my life. I let go of the plans I'd had for the last 15 years. I let go of feeling like God had forgotten about me.

Almost 10 years later...

My ex may have told me I don't have what it takes to be a good mother, but I single-handedly raised a funny, kind, and respectful young man in whom I've instilled strong and positive morals and values. He is an aide for my 2nd grade Religious Education and is the great role model I've always believed he could be. He's earned all A's since first grade; and recently completed his first year of High School with honors, ranked #1 of almost 200 students in his grade.

I am a Life Strategist and my clients turn to me to show them how to manage stress and prevent burnout. The recently divorced reach out to me for breakup recovery support where I listen to their needs and lay out a plan to help them on their way to healing their hearts. I am a parenting expert for several popular online communities where I help moms and dads across the globe raise happy, responsible, respectful, and motivated children.

If my life followed my original plans, I'm certain I would not have gained the knowledge, experience, and passion to contribute in the healing of those who God brings my way every day. The devil may have knocked me down to my knees, but that's when God came to save me. He needed me to surrender so that I would be open to live my true purpose for which He created me. Because of the pain and rejection I have experienced, I am able to find joy in almost everything, my happiness bursts from the bottom of my soul, I love fiercely with every fiber of my being, I am confident beyond doubt in my parenting abilities, and I've been blessed with the gift of compassionate empathy and the ability to help comfort those who are hurting.

I would not trade these for anything.

"Thank you, God for redirecting me and guiding me back to where I am meant to be. Please continue to bless me with love, clarity, and strength to live your purpose for me."

APPLICATION

You are a precious child of God and He loves you more than you can possibly comprehend.

Every person serves a very real purpose in your life. Not everyone will be on your side and that's OK because we all see things based on our individual experiences and how those things make us feel about ourselves. It's up to you to identify the lessons and blessings in those you cross paths with, and choose what energy you want to fill your space with.

Plans change but there's always a different path. Open your heart and mind to it or you will be miserable all your life. Perhaps God is saying "No" because He's saving you from harm... or more often than not, He has something much better than what you could have ever planned for yourself.

With God on your side, there is NOTHING you cannot overcome. If the hardship is caused by someone else, remember that it is NOT a punishment to you. Trust that God will ALWAYS give you the strength to pull through and the clarity to identify the blessing in it. You need only to climb out of your stubbornness and self-pity, accept His help, and follow through. Focus on God and His promises to you. God has GUARANTEED your win. Claim it.

PRAYER

God, my desire is Inner Peace and to feel your love and presence in my heart. I leave the result of this situation in your hands. I know you love me and I trust in your plans for me. May YOUR will be done.

DAILY DECLARATION

Remember God's immeasurable love for us, and trust that He is always on our side. Everything will work out for your best. #FaithIntoAbundance

MEET CARMEN SAKURAI

Carmen is a Life Strategist, Teacher, and Advice Columnist with over 20 years of education, experiences, and intuitions in Mental Decluttering, Breakup/Divorce Recovery, Stress Reduction, and Burnout Prevention.

She is a contributor for Piccolo Universe founded by Ricky Martin for parents and caregivers to share parenting advice; a featured expert for SheKnows, a community that inspires and empowers women to explore and pursue their passions; and Lifehack, a premier productivity and lifestyle blog.

In addition to mothering, running her business, experimenting in the kitchen, and living la vida loca, Carmen volunteers as a 1st and 2nd grade religious education teacher and high school youth group leader.

She currently resides in Las Vegas, NV with her son Joshua and their cat Jordyn.

CONTACT CARMEN

WEBSITE
CarmenSakurai.com
MarketingChick.com
NinjaMomDiaries.com
GirlPlusFood.com

FACEBOOK
Facebook.com/CarmenSakurai

LINKEDIN
LinkedIn.com/in/CarmenSakurai

TWITTER
@CarmenSakurai

DAY 3

BASEBALL, BOOZE AND HER IMAGINARY FRIEND JESUS

ROBERT THORNTON

"Many are the plans in the mind of a man, but it is the purpose of the Lord that will stand."

Proverbs 19:21

Ever since birth, the only thing I thought about was playing Major League Baseball.

It commanded my every waking moment and I'm pretty sure all my dreams were about baseball. As a kid, I would bring my glove and a ball with me everywhere I went...and I do mean everywhere, trips to the grocery store with my mom, to the lake, on long road trips, to our Christmas parties at my Grandmother's house. EVERYWHERE.

Religion was not something that was discussed in my household growing up. I can recall going to church one time as a young child. My Mom took me to a Catholic church and the Priest was telling people how they were going to Hell. I remember holding my Mom's hand as we left and she looked down at me and said, "We're never coming back here again." I remember nodding vigorously in agreement.

I just kept my focus on baseball, and everything else fell far behind my love and commitment for the game.

Fast forward to me being 27 years old and getting invited to Spring Training with the Sioux City Explorers.

When I got there, I found there was no place to live and the owner of the team had me staying in the visitor's clubhouse. During the offseason I had begun training with a new guy and he loved to throw the football to build arm strength. I agreed, but looking back believe it is this throwing that led to me walking away from the game I loved.

That spring, a pain started to develop in my elbow that was so intense that every day I was taking five or six 1000 milligram Ibuprofens. As you can guess, I started having a lot of stomach pain. I went to the doctor and they ran some tests, took some scans and told me I had a partial tear in my Ulnar Collateral Ligament, which meant I would need surgery if I wanted to continue playing ball.

I went back to the clubhouse and did a long night of soul searching. The surgery and following rehab would be between 12-16 months. That meant I would be another year older, and even farther away from reaching my goal of playing in the MLB.

I asked myself if I gave the game all I had, and had worked as hard as possible to make my dreams a reality. My answer was "yes."

So I headed home, enrolled at Arizona State University, and got a bartending job. I was 27 years old and had never had even a drop of alcohol in my body. This all changed very quickly.

I lost my identity. All I wanted to do was to drink so much each night that I wouldn't think of my failure to reach the majors. Sadly, I got blackout drunk every night for three years.

Then a new girl, Denise, started at work and I overheard her tell coworkers she was "a believer" to which I stopped and said "A believer in what?"

She then told me about her faith in God. I proceeded to mock her every single time I saw her, asking her things like, "How is your imaginary friend Jesus today?"

But she never responded in anger. Not once.

One Saturday night Denise joined us out at the bar. I was completely hammered and said to her "I'm going to church with you tomorrow." Denise instantly got this surprised (and a little terrified) look on her face. But she then told me when and where.

The next morning, still reeking of Gin, I put on a suit and met her at church. Her facial expressions indicated she did not expect me to show. We sat down and the pastor began to take lessons from the Bible and apply them to his life. From his first story, my life was forever changed and I accepted God into my life and fully believe that Jesus died for my sins.

THE LESSON OF FAITH

The main lesson I learned from that first trip, something that has stayed with me and helps me in my time of doubt, is that God has a plan. He knows more than me, and I have to have complete faith in Him.

I was mad at the world when I could no longer play baseball. God then put me on a path that led to starting my first business that is completely focused on making this world a better place for those with special needs. That took all the anger and sadness from me.

If I had made it to the big leagues, would I be helping people the way I am helping them now? I doubt it.

This also helps me when bad events occur in my life and in the world, I just keep my faith in Him and try and always find a lesson I can learn from the negative events.

INTO ABUNDANCE

This lesson helps me in running Paper Clouds Apparel. I learned that when you start a business with only the two dimes you have in your pocket, you must believe God put the idea in your head for a reason.

I believe that helping others is why God put me on this Earth. So, when there are hard times, and they are plenty of them, I look to Him for the lesson in it.

I also believe that if I continue to work hard and do the right thing that God will find ways to reward me. I don't always mean in a monetary way though. He will put people in my path who need help. He will put people in my path who can help me. It is just a beautiful thing to know my purpose and know He loves me.

APPLICATION

I not only use this lesson in my business life but in every second of my personal life as well. You can too!

Life is much better when you learn to have faith in Him and his decisions as they pertain to your life. We don't always know what is right, sometimes it can be hard to have complete faith in Him, but you have to find it.

I used to struggle when I would hear about a young child dying from something like cancer. Now I just have faith that maybe the death of that child will inspire their brother or sister to find the cure for this terrible disease. It can be difficult to accept but it will make your life a lot happier if you put your life in His hands and just believe he knows best.

PRAYER

God, thank You for allowing me to see another day and to learn how I can share Your love for me with others. Thank You for keeping my loved ones safe and letting them see all you have created for us. I pray You will let me and my loved ones see another day and another chance to love you more.

DAILY DECLARATION

We are not wise enough to question His decisions. We need to always keep our faith in Him and learn the lessons He has laid out before us. #FaithIntoAbundance

MEET ROBERT THORNTON

Originally born with a primary focus to play Major League Baseball, Robert Thornton's life took a serious detour when he was injured and could no longer pursue his passion.

Lost for three years before allowing God into his life, Robert is now focused on making this world a better place for those with special needs and for the homeless. To see how this man is changing the world for these two communities, Google his two businesses, Paper Clouds Apparel and Cloud Covered Streets.

CONTACT ROBERT

Paper Clouds Apparel & Cloud Covered Streets

WEBSITE
PaperCloudsApparel.com
CloudCoveredStreets.org

FACEBOOK
Facebook.com/PaperCloudsApparel
Facebook.com/CloudCoveredStreets

TWITTER
@papercloudsPCA

INSTAGRAM
@papercloudsapparel
@cloudcoveredstreets

LINKEDIN
LinkedIn.com/in/Robert-Thornton-42b3b755

DAY 4

MY PEARL OF GREAT PRICE

JILLIAN QUINN

"For now we see through a glass, darkly; but then face to face: now I know in part, but then shall I know even also as I am known."

1 Corinthians 13

Life can shatter your heart into a million pieces in one sickening second. When I was in my early thirties, I was in my sixth month of pregnancy with my third child and thrilled to be expanding my family. I had traded in my car for a minivan, decorated the nursery and had just made arrangements to take time off from my college teaching. I had made it through the first few miserable months of morning-noon-and-night sickness and was at that stage of magical end-of-second-trimester bliss. My skin was glowing, my hair was shining and I was filling out my maternity clothes with a baby-bump that nurtured inside me a tiny baby girl whose every movement made me smile and whose nightly hiccups kept me awake.

One beautiful April morning, I drove to my midwife's office for a routine pre-natal visit. Teddy, my little boy, was old enough to be excited to hear his baby sister's heartbeat. My going-on-two-year-old daughter, Mia, had been speaking in complete sentences for months and definitely wanted to hear "her baby." We were a happy little trio surrounding the little life we loved already. I felt more than blessed and filled with an unspeakable love for my son and daughter and the little life inside of me.

At the office, when the midwife couldn't find my baby's heartbeat, I tried to push down my panic and believe my midwife's assurances that the baby was likely just facing away from the stethoscope. I tried to remain calm while they ushered me into the hospital's sonogram suite to see what was going on. As I lay there, I kept one hand on my toddler and the other on my heart, which felt like it was going to explode. When the technician wouldn't tell me anything, I tried to believe that the look I saw in her eyes was something other than what I knew it to be. But then my midwife came in. I will never forget her words. She said "Jillian, I am so very sorry. Her heart has stopped and we have no idea why. I'm terribly sorry, but she's gone."

I sat up and lifted each of my two tiny children onto the table and explained that their baby sister had gone to heaven. I held them and answered their questions and tried to explain things in a way that they would understand. On the surface, I remained calm. But inside, I felt my heart not exploding as I had thought it might but imploding, collapsing in upon itself. I was so far along in my pregnancy that had to be induced and go through labor and delivery of my precious baby girl, knowing she'd be gone when I first saw her or have a major surgery and then deal with that aftermath. I was now beyond the realm of all thought. I felt as though I was watching everything unfold from above.

When we finally arrived at home, I asked my husband to take the kids out of the house and in the privacy of my bedroom, I cried so hard and for so long that I broke all the blood vessels in my eyes—even some across my cheeks. My entire body ached with grief and anger and loss. I was profoundly and acutely aware of my baby girl's body still within mine and I felt torn apart; I needed to let her go and I also couldn't let her go. I was sick to my very soul.

Alone in my room—my dead baby inside me—I experienced what some refer to as a "dark night of the soul." At that moment, I could no longer feel God with me. The pain I felt was so visceral, I felt I'd been punched in the solar plexus. I didn't know how to carry on without the choice of carrying my baby. I couldn't cope with the intensity of feeling that kept knocking me down in successive waves and I couldn't draw anything more than a ragged breath, such was my grief and despair. I felt like I was drowning and part of me just wanted to go under. I realized that I needed to let go not only of my darling, tiny girl but also of all control. I needed to let God carry us both through this. I needed God to carry me through this valley of the shadow of death.

THE LESSON OF FAITH

I began to pray. I fell first to my knees and then flat out on the wood floor. I prayed aloud. I prayed for I don't know how long...and as I prayed, I again felt God's presence. I felt His solace. I heard His words, telling me that not only would I survive this heartbreak but that I would find meaning and purpose within and from it, if I walked in faith. My own perspective was limited by the heart-wrenching grief I felt but through the limitless perspective God afforded me, I was able to whisper a faint "We shall see..."

Three years later, my husband and I traveled to Southern China to adopt a fourteen-month-old baby girl from an orphanage filled with beautiful baby girls whose birth mothers lived in a world of cruel circumstances and unimaginable pressures. When I met my daughter, she had never had a bath, was in need of medical attention and slept with no mattress in a metal crib in a sweltering room with dozens of other babies. My daughter is now twelve and she is my pearl of great price, ransomed from a sea of red tape and an ocean of loss. She is my daughter and I am her mother *only* because in my past, I lost a daughter and in her past, she lost a mother. I look into her eyes and see the manifestation of a God who is greater than our greatest losses and our greatest heartbreaks. Remembering this, I sink to my knees in gratitude for all of the moments of my life—even those that were the most brutal and the most shattering. Actually, I am especially grateful for those moments, for a broken heart is an open heart...a heart ever-more-open to God.

INTO ABUNDANCE

A short time after adopting our daughter, I was offered a book deal from a highly respected New York publisher. The book's topic was fine but not the one I felt God was calling me to write. I heard over and over again that I'd "be crazy" to walk away from such a deal. But in my heart, I felt myself closing the door on this project. There was no other book deal awaiting me anywhere and many advised me that this was a "next step" that I'd regret not taking. I trusted in the still, small voice within my heart.

Just two months later, I was standing on the beach in San Diego—watching my little ones playing in the surf—when I got a voicemail message and an email, both offering me a six-figure advance for the *exact* book I felt God calling me to write. I did not have to struggle to receive this offer from the world's largest and most prestigious publisher; I'd sent an email inquiry and proposal to an editor I did not know and knew it would likely sit in a slush-pile, possibly forever.

I sent no inquiries or proposals to any other editors or publishers—just the single one, and it was unsolicited and un-agented. I just sent it out in blind faith and whispered a faint "We shall see." I received that six-figure offer for the very book I felt profoundly called to write within ONE HOUR of sending the email. And the rest, as they say, is history.

My book was a bestseller and the rest of my career took off. I claim no credit, other than showing up and walking in faith. God created that book and that abundance. Our God is an awesome God...awesome beyond our limited imaginations of what is possible.

APPLICATION

It's important to remember that seemingly "bad" things really can and do happen to every human being and to virtually every career or business. To expect otherwise is to misunderstand the mysterious ways of God. Know that you *will* face adversity and that when it strikes, God has not abandoned you.

Continue to walk in faith—even through the blackest night—and this will lead you to the destiny God has planned for you. And it is a different, bigger and better one than you could ever imagine for yourself. When something seems to be the very worst thing you can imagine happening, keep the faith and whisper your own faint "We shall see."

PRAYER

Dear All-Knowing and All-Giving God, You knew me before I took form and know the innermost workings of my heart. You know how profoundly I need Your solace, healing and grace right now as my heart struggles to bear this weight. Oh, Lord, this cup is too great to bear without Your grace and strength. Please come into my shattered heart and begin to bind up my brokenness. Dearest God, shine Your light upon this dark path I now walk. I through myself upon Your mercy and compassion and know that through You, the impossible is effortless and no miracle is beyond Your power. Thank You for the countless gifts you bestow upon those faithful to You and also for the faithfulness You show to all who love and follow You. Amen.

DAILY DECLARATION

Continue to walk in faith—even through the blackest night—and this will lead you to the destiny God has planned for you. #FaithIntoAbundance

MEET JILLIAN QUINN

Jillian Quinn's calling is helping people take life's heart-breaking hits and turn them into soul-making victories. As an Associate Minister at The Interfaith Temple in New York City and through her workshops and classes, Jillian has reached thousands of people around the country with her inspiring and practical prescription for finding happiness beyond heartache.

Jillian is the best-selling author of the self-help book The Secrets of the Bulletproof Spirit: How to Bounce Back from Life's Hardest Hits, published by Random House in February of 2009. Her work has been featured on The Early Show on CBS, The Discovery Channel, The Pat McMahon Show, in magazines such as Self, Personal Excellence, and Savvy Family, and on countless radio shows around the country, including The God Show and programming on National Public Radio affiliate stations. She lives with her husband and three children in Millbrook, New York.

CONTACT JILLIAN

WEBSITE
JillianQuinn.com

FACEBOOK
Facebook.com/Jillian.Quinn.5

DAY 5

FROM ASHES TO GOD'S GLORY

MIKE "MOUNTAINMAN" LAMBORNE

"And my God will meet all your needs according to the riches of his glory in Christ Jesus."

Philippians 4:19

After many years of hard work, and many, many 20-hour days, my wife, Shirley, and I developed a very successful art business, which consisted of pinstriping and hand painted murals on motorcycles. We would follow the rally circuit starting with Daytona Bike Week in March and ending up with the Christian Motorcyclists Association International Rally in mid October.

At 3:10 A.M. on January 28, 2006, God woke Shirley. She sat straight up in bed and said, "The house is on fire!" She awakened me immediately and when I looked out our bedroom window upon the snow-covered hillside, I saw the glow of orange on the snow. I was up in a flash and grabbed my jeans, took no time for socks or shirt. I woke our son, Michael, who in turn grabbed his dog who was hiding under the bed. We ran down stairs for my shop, which was attached to the side of the house.

There was no smoke in the house, therefore no alarms when off. I could hear crackling in the walls between the house and the shop. As I entered the shop, I saw flames on that wall.

Shirley called 911. We knew not to expect help for 20-30 minutes because of how remote our area is. Not only do we live on the side of a mountain, three miles off the main highway on a single lane road, but so do the volunteer firefighters we would be waiting for. Other fire companies had to be called in to prevent the fire from spreading and they were over thirty miles away – and across the mountain.

After my son tossed the dog out to safety, he was right behind me heading for the shop. During our 'off season' throughout the winter months, our clients from all over the world ship us bike parts to paint. We had several projects in the shop I had painted and others were waiting to be painted.

Shirley moved our vehicle out of the way and my son and I got most of the bikes and bike parts out of the shop before the fire had taken over the entire garage.

Shirley called our daughter, Michelle, who lived about a mile away, to let her know about the fire. That was 3:16 AM – just a mere 6 minutes from the time Shirley woke – and when she looked back at the house it was entirely engulfed in flames.

There was nothing more we could do except to try to get our tour bus – which was parked about a foot away from the shop – out of the driveway to safety. It was below freezing and that ole Detroit had been sitting for almost three cold months and the batteries were just about dead.

I yelled at my son to see if it would start. He turned the key but all he got was a small grunt. He prayed, "Please God start this thing!" He hit the key again and amazingly, it fired up immediately. It took several minutes to build up the air pressure to release the brakes so it could be moved.

When I jumped in to move it, the rear tires just spun on ice. I let it drift forward a few inches and by that time it was just about a foot from the shooting flames. I could not hear my wife and son screaming for me to get out of the bus and let it go because the flames were shooting up over the front of the bus.

I nailed the accelerator and was able to spin back off the ice. Miraculously, the bus, whose name was, "Expression of Faith" took off in reverse. The road was one narrow lane, curved slightly and went uphill at a fairly steep incline. The drop off on my right side was 50 feet down into a hollow. I was blinded by the light of the fire in front of me and I just prayed. The bus went backward up the hill and went around a sharp curve into a driveway three to four hundred yards away.

I got out of the bus and walked back to the blazing house. Then I just stopped and stared at it from 50-60 yards away with temperatures in the 20's and it dawned on me that I didn't even have a shirt on. This is when I realized that all we had from 31 years of marriage was gone. I stared at the scene and the words to a Ray Boltz's song came to me, "It was in the night, during the storms of our lives that God reveals His love is real."

I was totally overcome by the most amazing peace and calm that I had ever experienced. Everybody was ok, and the rest was just stuff!

INTO ABUNDANCE

The word spread quickly that our house was completely burned to the ground. Shirley's Dad lived next door. He opened his house to us and said we should use it as our own. Friends, Churches and family flocked in with donations of money, food, clothes and our daughter Kathy and her husband Ricky, who live three hours away, showed up with an entire pickup full of all brand name essentials that we normally used. We received cards full of money from all over the US, many with names we didn't even recognize, but we knew they had to be our customers. What a blessing!

It was only one month till we had to leave for the bike rallies to paint more bikes.

We had lost everything. Paint, supplies, photo catalogs of our work for display, everything was gone.

But God was at work! UPS ran every day bringing us painting supplies from other Pinstriper friends from all over the US and Canada. A friend in North Carolina got on the GWRRA motorcycle chat room and had photos of hundreds of bikes I had painted sent to him and he put them into catalogs for us. Even the paint manufacturers sent us cartons of paint and supplies.

When we got to Daytona, we were back in business and praising God for how He brought us through this fire and blessed us beyond measure. There were an abundance of bikers and customers that flocked in our tent, where we did our painting, to console us and told us how sorry they were for our loss. By the time we had told our story and how God had given us the peace and joy we felt after the fire, they were saying how they were blessed and lifted up because of our faith.

APPLICATION

We had a pretty strong faith in Jesus Christ for quite a few years. He guided us into this business where I was able to use my God-given talent to make a living doing what I loved. But looking back, there were some worldly things I wasn't ready to give up.

Two months before the fire, my mother had given me, out of 6 kids, our two hundred year old family bible. I was pretty shook up over it and was still trying to hang on to that loss. Shirley was praying one night several days after the fire. God told her to tell me to let it go, the Bible was so old and fragile we couldn't even turn the pages. He revealed that it was no longer of any use for Him.

So what is this all about? Jesus fills you with the power of His Holy Spirit, who immediately lifts you up out of the adversity and through it all that still small voice tells you it's going to be all right (1 Kings 19:12). That peace of God that surpasses all understanding totally takes over you and you know that you know that God has led you through this (Philippians 4:19).

When we looked back into those ashes, we knew that all we lost was worldly stuff. You know that God has a greater plan for your life and for your business, which has become a ministry.

The abundance, strength and success of a business is not in the bank account, it's in your love for God which fills your heart and overflows to everyone around you.

We learned through this experience that we needed to always put God first in our daily lives and in our business. Always remember (Colossians 3:17) "And whatever you do in word or deed, do all in the name of the Lord Jesus, giving thanks to God the Father through Him."

PRAYER

Lord God, you are an awesome God. We give you all the praise, honor and glory. We thank you for your love, your salvation and patience with us. We thank you for the power of your most HOLY Spirit, who guides us in all that we do in our work and our daily lives, in Jesus' name, Amen.

DAILY DECLARATION

The abundance, strength and success of a business is not in the bank account, it's in your love for God which fills your heart and overflows to everyone around you. #FaithIntoAbundance

MEET MIKE "THE MOUNTAINMAN" LAMBORNE

Mountainman Mike Lamborne has been drawing and painting most of his life. He grew up on a small farm in Maryland where he worked at a Blacksmith shop and studied Agriculture at Maryland University, thinking there was no future in art. Later, he married Shirley and moved to West Virginia where they farmed, ran a parts store and welded in coalmines. After years of struggling they moved to Northern Virginia and started a trucking business. That's where they were introduced to motorcycle rallies. They moved back to the mountains of West Virginia and with his old CB handle of "Mountainman" they now travel nine months out of the year working the motorcycle circuit.

Mountainman uses a hand painted technique with airbrushed highlights for his murals at the rallies. He is well known for his detailed work. His fine line pinstriping and graphics are hand painted.

During the "Desert Storm War" he did an ink drawing to benefit the USO. Prints went to former President Bush, Secretary of State Richard Cheney, General Norman Swartzcoft, Oliver North, Senator John Warner, General and Military personal the world over. The POW's and wounded of Desert Storm were presented one of the prints at a special dinner in Pentagon City, near Washington, DC.

CONTACT MIKE

WEBSITE
mountainmanart.com

FACEBOOK
Facebook.com/MikeLamborne

DAY 6

PRO ATHLETE LIFESTYLE HARDENED MY HEART

DAVID NORRIE

"Be sober, be vigilant; because your adversary the devil, as a roaring lion, walketh about, seeking whom he may devour."

1 Peter 5:8

For as long as I can remember, I loved sports. I was the first one knocking on a friend's door early Saturday morning, hoping I didn't wake their parents, but anxious to get to the park and start playing football or baseball or whatever the season was.

For as long as I can remember, I always loved God. My family was the first in church early on Sunday morning, dressed up and anxious to be inspired by the priest and partake in the service.

As I got older, I realized I was good at sports but not great, and after a horrible car accident on the way home from football practice in 11th grade, it wasn't long before I knew that sports wouldn't be a part of my future in the way that I'd hoped.

As I got older, I realized I was a good Christian but not great and after I graduated college I slowly began drifting away from church and it wasn't long before I allowed Jesus to drift out of my life in a way I had always hoped He wouldn't.

My thirst for sports landed me a job in journalism, covering the very athletes I grew up wishing I could be. It allowed me to go places and meet people that any diehard fan would dream of.

At the same time, my thirst for women and the athlete lifestyle led me farther and farther away from Jesus. It made it acceptable for me to go places and meet women any gregarious young man would dream of.

Here's the problem. On the surface everything seemed great and appeared to be going in the right direction, but underneath I was lonely, unhappy and unfulfilled. As a journalist, I'd always kept a journal. And from time to time, I'd look back on my entries and realize that though the years passed, my problems did not. In terms of my career, there was always stress over work that didn't pay much and had little job security. In my personal life, there were plenty of entries that spoke of women who didn't give much but had plenty of insecurities.

And while the job titles and women's names always changed, one thing remained consistent... Jesus was always there. Not where he should've been, certainly not in the center, yet always present, peeking around the corners every other page or so. Those five letters, His name, were my go-to when things looked really bleak. Those five letters I wrote, sometimes legibly and sometimes scratched after coming home filled with alcohol but feeling empty from a night on the town.

The job turned stale as the allure of interviewing the big names in the NFL was gone. But even worse was my love life. I was done. I was throwing the towel in on women, having ended a relationship with yet another one who loved herself more than she could love anybody else. So I said "That's it."

I accepted a job as an editor of a magazine working for a publisher, who was of all things, a former professional football player. That week I opened my journal and said, "Jesus I'm tired and I'm lonely and I know I've been terrible at picking women, but please send me somebody I could pour my heart into. Please send me an Angel." I even signed it...David.

Then the story came. My publisher said, "I need you to do an article on this girl who just won a fitness competition. Here's her contact information."

"Great." I thought, "Just what I need, another self-centered woman." I went to the interview telling myself, "Don't even look at her. Do your job and take notes with your head down."

Thirty minutes into the interview, we were finished. But the conversation was just getting started. Her name was Angelike (almost Angel-Like) and she spoke to me a lot about God and Jesus.

That conversation begot another and another and another. Although Angelike and I began to take things to another level, my relationship with Jesus wasn't moving at the same pace. Until one day it happened. I was reluctant to give up "my life with my boys" on the weekends and some bad habits and that was it, she was gone.

A stubborn and hardened heart is no place to cultivate love and mine was as hardened as they come. Hers, luckily, was full of kindness, patience and love. She came to me and said "David, the last thing the devil wants is for two people who love Jesus to come together and create a family. He will do everything he can to come between us and if you don't realize that then you're a fool."

THE LESSON OF FAITH

From that moment on, everything changed. I realized that indeed the devil would try hard and often to come between us and that a healthy relationship in God was what is necessary. Angelike and I began studying the bible together. We got married shortly after in God's house and with him as the center of our ceremony.

Her opening me to the Word alerted me not only to the devil's intentions but my stubbornness to realize that whether business or love there is only one answer, and Jesus is it. In our marriage I've noticed when we've prayed together, things are really good, and when we get distracted away from the Word, things get shaky. But we always identify it and make sure He is at the center.

INTO ABUNDANCE

About a year into our marriage I left journalism and my wife left her career in sales and we began a home-based business together. Like marriage, our business was challenging at times, but like our relationship we realized when we put God in the middle and focused on loving others that we would be rewarded.

I had always felt like a square peg in a round hole my entire career, never finding the perfect fit. But here we were, five years into our marriage, four years into our business, when we made our first million dollars. The path led me to the woman who led me to the business where I could use all the gifts God blessed me with to enhance the lives of those around me. We decided, like our marriage, that we wouldn't allow God to paly a small role but rather praise him for everything he put in our path. In turn, he has given us a large platform to use our voices and we promised Him, way before our good fortune, that we'd always use it to glorify him.

Here's the kicker, as our business grows, I continue to run into former athletes whom I end up bringing into the business and into the Word. Two of which have made a huge impact. The first, a former big league pitcher, has probably done more for my faith than anybody since my wife, educating me in the Word and making me thirst for Jesus like never before. The other, a massive, mountain of a man, and former NFL player, came to me one day, asking for lunch. Halfway through lunch, I said, "Hey man, what is this meeting really about? It's not about work." He responded, "You're right, it's about God, I see how you speak of him and want to know more."

Now, the former pitcher, lineman and sportswriter get together every week (with our women) to do bible study. Funny how God works.

APPLICATION

It's always about God's time. At 36, I was in a dead end job with no hope for a good woman in sight. By 39 I'd literally found my Angel and we were working on, we didn't know at the time, what was a multi-million dollar business.

Never give up on prayer or God and he will always come with the right thing when the time is right. I strongly encourage all couples to read the word together and keep Him at the center of everything you do. No relationship is perfect but the answers are right there in the book.

As for business, be a visible man of God. I feel as if our cars are in the front of our house, our gold watches are in front of our handshake and our egos are often in front of our conversations. But tucked away somewhere way in the back is our faith, neatly folded in the shirt closet for Sundays only. That has to change.

PRAYER

It takes a man to stand up for God, and God to stand as the bond between a man and a woman.

Jesus, we walk through the woods seeking a path that isn't always clear. We ask that you guide us in our daily lives and bring our bonds as Christians and those of husband and wife tighter each day. May we love one another as you love the Church and may you bless us with safety and wisdom so that we may continue to do your work.

DAILY DECLARATION

When you take God out of your home and your relationship, the devil will always try to sneak in. Be vigilant and speak the Word each day. #FaithIntoAbundance

MEET DAVID NORRIE

David Norrie is a Transformational Coach specializing in helping individuals tap into their true personality in a way that helps them excel in both their professional and personal lives.

For the past four years, David has worked as a business coach for one of the largest network marketing companies in the world. While doing that, he saw a need for more intensive training in helping people market themselves in a social media driven marketplace. That led to the creation of Socially Speaking, an 8-week interactive virtual training course that takes groups of men and women from different fields and helps them develop their stories and become better listeners as well as more influential speakers.

Norrie has spoken to large audiences all over the country and is most passionate about God, marriage, family and capitalism.

He spent over 20 years in journalism, most of which came as a columnist, penning articles on how to have a healthier body and relationship. He draws on humor and his experience as a husband and father to get across his message that God is indeed laying out a path for each of us and its our responsibility to be stewards of his message and create a better future for the next generation.

He and his wife, Angelike, run their home-based business out of Arizona and believe their ministry includes reaching out to couples who want to work together and coaching them on how to make their marriage coincide with their business.

CONTACT DAVID

WEBSITE
SociallySpeaking.club

FACEBOOK
Facebook.com/David.Norrie.96

LINKEDIN
LinkedIn.com/in/David-Norrie-b26831114

INSTAGRAM
@davidnorrie6

DAY 7

PRETZELS OF FAITH

SCOTT JONES AND BRIAN KRIDER

"So then faith cometh by hearing, and hearing by the word of God."

Romans 10:17

All stories have to start somewhere. I am glad that I am able to say this one starts with doing something to build the Kingdom of Christ. We all hope and wish that our good stories start that way, and while not all do, we are so thankful when the stories with bad starts turn out good in the end. However, it is really great when our good start ups to stories end as even better stories.

So as this story goes, I was doing ministry visitations with a guy named Cory and we got lost in the heart of Amish country Indiana. We finally figured out we where close to a friend of Cory's named Ben. Ben was an Amish guy that had a bakery, and Cory thought we could get a cookie or some other fresh baked product if we visited Ben's bakery. It was here that I met Ben and gained not only a cookie or two, but also a really good friend.

I should introduce myself. My name is Scott Jones. I am fortunate to now to own a business with Ben (Miller) called Ben's Soft Pretzels. This story is not about me, and it's not even about Ben. This story is about the transformation we have seen in our third business partner, Brian Krider, over the last eight years.

After Ben and I met, we became very good friends and started to have social functions with our families. We enjoyed having times of bible studies together and comparing our faith walks. My family is non-denominational while Ben's family was Amish. Our wives, Candy and Elizabeth, became good friends and remain that way today. The differences in our heritage and culture made for great bible learning opportunities for both families.

While my wife and I were enjoying building a great relationship with Ben and his family, we were also getting to know my friend Brian and his family a little better. Brian and I previously worked together in the RV industry for a period of time, as we started a business together that made and sold trailers, grilled chicken and did resale of a number of items. We enjoyed of the pursuit of these business ventures but none of them really brought us a lot of satisfaction.

After introducing Brian and Ben to one another, we all became friends. It didn't take long after that for Ben to introduce his wonderful baked products to Brian and me. This led to all three of us meeting on a regular basis to discuss a future partnership, and eventually led to Brian and me selling the Amish baked goods company to a number of grocery stores and Sam's Clubs in our local area.

One day after a hunting trip, Ben offered to buy lunch at his new bakery stand that offered pretzels, which turned out to be the best soft pretzel I had ever eaten in my life. I was excited to share this product with Brian who also fell head over heels in love with the fresh hot soft pretzels.

After our waistlines expanded a few inches, we decided that it was time to grow our business. Ben, Brian, and I sat down and worked out an idea that Brian had to start a business built just around the pretzel.

In 2008, we launched our first pretzel store and the business did great. We launched the second store in 2009, and soon after we started a partnership with the University of Notre Dame. From there the business took off. However, it's the rest of the story that really helps bring the matter into focus.

As I mentioned earlier, Ben and I held bible studies on a regular basis. This eventually led to Ben and his wife leaving the Amish faith. This was a big step in their lives as this would cause them to be no longer accepted by their families, which is referred to as shunning in the Amish faith.

This led to an interesting conversation between Brian and myself.

Somewhere in year two of our business, Brian asked me about Ben and Elizabeth becoming saved and leaving the Amish church. He asked me what exactly we meant when we referred to ourselves as "saved."

So I took this opportunity to share all that I knew about salvation with Brian. He said, "Okay, so basically it is all the 'stuff' I learned when I was a kid." One thing that I didn't mention earlier was that Brian was raised and is still a practicing Catholic.

About three years into our growth we hit a wall. It seemed like we were doing well in our stores but we just weren't able to always make the right decisions. Money was going out as fast as it came in. We had big plans, but it seemed they were going down like a sinking ship. The original business plan we wrote was very aggressive and was outlined for not one or two stores, but for over 1,000. We needed something to change. Then change came along.

Brian informed me that he was going to a men's retreat with his church. He was excited to hear someone share their witness story, but nervous since he had never experienced anything like this before.

Our business really changed after this trip. Brian came back a different man. He asked me if I remembered the conversation that we had a year or so before about salvation. I said, "Of course I do." He told me that he really knew what it meant to be saved now, as he had a revelation during the men's retreat. Brian recognized Jesus as his personal savior for years but just came to recognize Him in a personal way in his life.

Brian ran the day-to-day operations of our business at that time and because of this, our business changed. The attitudes of employees changed. The belief and the power in prayer as the three of us moved in the same stream with our faiths made all the difference.

This renewal of Brian's faith became evident in his speech, actions and in our business. Our employees changed whether they knew it or not. This isn't to say Brian was a bad guy before; he was far from it. It just that the well that he dipped into for his source of peace, wisdom and strength was different. He saw the need of his relationship with Christ with renewed eyes. This caused for relationships with employees to be renewed and for the business to change – all for the better.

This isn't to say that we didn't have our problems still. Instead of letting bitterness, strife and anxiety work its way into our business we started praying and believing for God's best for us.

The greatest part is that our business went from the red back into the black. We were able to start growing and have been blessed with good sustainable growth since.

THE LESSON OF FAITH

A scripture that really applies to this is Romans 10:17, *"So then faith cometh by hearing, and hearing by the word of God"*.

The Word of God is so crucial to our faith walk. John 1:1 says, "In the beginning was the Word, and the Word was with God, and the Word was God." John 1:14 goes further and says, "And the Word was made flesh, and dwelt among us, (and we beheld His glory, the glory as of the only begotten of the Father), full of grace and truth."

To really know Jesus and to exercise our faith in the fullest degree with him, we need to know Him. We need to leave the confines of any religious boundaries and see Jesus as our confidant, source of peace, our tower of refuge and our friend.

Do you think of Jesus that way? That He is your friend.

The weekend that Brian spent with his men's group bore witness to these facts:

1. Jesus was his friend.

2. He could enter into a personal relationship with Jesus and own that relationship.

3. That it was direct relationship between Brian and Jesus.

4. That the veil that separated God and man was rent from top to bottom when Jesus gave His life for us, and it gave opportunity for us to have a direct relationship with Jesus.

We now have the opportunity to petition Jesus directly in His name for our needs, for our comfort and for our peace. We also know beyond of a shadow of doubt that our eternity will be spent with our friend Jesus.

INTO ABUNDANCE

We were very blessed by God's unseen hand as he positioned Ben, Brian and me all in the right places at the right time to form a friendship and ultimately a business. We have seen God's blessings and experience them daily by having a truly excellent product that was crafted with faith and love by Ben and his wife Elizabeth.

We work hard and we work smart, we know that this is a must in order to become successful.

With all of us flowing in the same stream in our faith and our relationship with the Lord it truly allowed us to recognize God's benevolent blessings in our lives and in our business. We have come to the mindset that if we can put God's kingdom first and seek His will, the rest will line up for us.

Time and time again we experience supernatural favor. Is it because Ben's Soft Pretzels is just that awesome of a business? I think we are pretty special, but we would only attribute the great favor to a loving friend we call Jesus. The Lord of our lives.

There are reasons that we experience abundance in our business. We believe that this is true because of cornerstones that we have recognized since the beginning of our business. It is also important that we all have the ability to understand that God is more than just a deity that we worship but that we KNOW He is our friend.

The cornerstones of our business have been:

1. The blessings of the Lord
2. Hard work
3. An excellent product

APPLICATION

By applying the principles of relationship to our business with Brian at the helm, he has been able to build great relationships. We have employees that have been in our business since we opened their respective stores. In addition to that, relationship building has allowed a young man under Brian's tutelage to flourish from a frontline employee to now working as our corporate trainer.

Again relationship building is key. First with the Lord and secondly with our neighbor. In Matthew 22:36-40, Jesus even answered those who asked what the most important commandment were, that Loving God was the most important commandment and the second was loving our neighbor. To do either one of those effectively requires good relationships.

If we make sure to exercise the first commandment without fail, then when we work with other individuals the second commandment will flow easy. It will be easy to love and it will be easy to build relationships. It will be easier to communicate. From this we can flow in what the Lord has prepared for us in our respective lives.

PRAYER

In your faithful and awesome name Jesus, we pray for your favor to continue to be with us.

DAILY DECLARATION

Never allow your issues to be greater than your relationships. Be a reflection and projection of Christ all of those we come into contact with. #FaithIntoAbundance

MEET SCOTT JONES & BRIAN KRIDER

SCOTT JONES

Scott Jones, CEO and Co-Founder, has led Ben's Soft Pretzels to become the fastest growing pretzel franchise in the US in only three short years since the company began franchising in 2013.

Scott's strong leadership skills and his heart for giving back and paying it forward have helped him to create a strong team, a simple process, and a thriving brand.

At the heart of each decision Scott makes is an intense desire to build a global business that serves delicious, twisted bites of happiness to all it serves, as well as providing a platform to bless others.

BRIAN KRIDER

CONTACT SCOTT AND BRIAN

Ben's Soft Pretzels

WEBSITE
BensPretzelsFranchising.com

FACEBOOK
Facebook.com/BensPretzels

LINKEDIN
LinkedIn.com/company/3043409

TWITTER
@benspretzels

INSTAGRAM
@benspretzels

DAY 8

SAVING A BABY IN A HOT CAR

LISA AVEDON

> *"For God is working in you; giving you the desire and the power to do what pleases Him."*
>
> *Romans 10:17*

Gifts are the skills and talents that come easily to us; those abilities that are second nature and fit so comfortably with who we are. From those gifts spring the desires that drive us to create, use, express and act so that our gifts can be fully realized.

Gifts can be tricky things sometimes. We can miss out on using all of our gifts because they're nestled within our very human complexity. Emotions, obligations, circumstances and fears can work to suppress and hide the best of gifts. Add God's gift of free-will into the mix, and it's no wonder we can lose sight of, and even completely miss, a few of the gifts we were born to use.

God uses a couple of my gifts in an interesting way.

Last summer, my daughter Ally and I were leaving a busy store. We had just stepped out into the beautiful 75-degree day when I heard a baby's cry. It came to me so clearly and distinctly that it was like an invisible lasso pulling me in its direction, guiding me directly to a minivan.

The minivan was parked with its windows cracked about an inch down, and inside was a baby. He was under a year old, strapped into his car seat and alone and scared. My instincts kicked in, and I immediately started talking to him, trying to sooth and comfort his fear, while I dialed 911. As the emergency operator answered, I stuck my fingers as far into the van's cracked window as I could, trying to determine how warm it was in the car. I saw that the baby wasn't sweating or flushed from being overheated, so I knew I didn't have to break a window for his safety.

A discussion with the Columbus city police, and then a face-to-face (peaceful!) confrontation with the baby's father ensued. When the entire drama of the baby's danger was past, I got into my car with Ally and sat for a moment to collect myself.

I always shake after finding and helping a baby.

You see, this was the fifth baby I've found locked in a car. Yes...you read that correctly...the FIFTH.

Ally turned to me and her eyes sparkled.

"Mom, that was so cool!" she said. "I didn't hear anything when we left the store, but you were like a heat-seeking missile locked on target! It was like God said 'Lisa's here. Send Lisa!'"

As crazy as that sounds, I think Ally's right. God uses me to help babies who are left in locked cars. He uses my two gifts of 'love and protectiveness for kids' and 'communication' in a way that benefits children who are in dangerous situations. That is cool!

THE LESSON OF FAITH

I'm able to use my gifts to help others, but when it came to using them for myself, I wasn't able to recognize them, and spent some time feeling lost and unclear about the direction of my life.

I was one of the millions who were laid off from my job. When that happened, it was as if my brain froze. While I prayed consistently..."God, please help me," I didn't open my heart and mind to His guidance. Fear managed to obscure my awareness of the gifts and desires that God had given me.

I was too focused on the messages from well-meaning family and friends who reminded me of my responsibilities and the need to get a 'real job'. There I was, a single mother with full custody of my three kids, a mortgage, a car payment and a dog. My level of responsibility was high, and I couldn't see a way to recognize and tap into what God had already given me: my gifts and my desires.

It wasn't until a friend reminded me that my gifts of communication, natural connection and business strategy were being sought after by people, that I realized I wanted to own my own marketing/public relations firm. In fact, when I thought about owning my own marketing/PR business, a joyous desire and excitement bubbled up within me. I realized that that joyous desire was both the direction and confirmation to take action. I acted on faith and started my business.

INTO ABUNDANCE

My digital marketing/PR firm, IdeaWorks, has been operating and growing for almost five years now. My business life and family life are intertwined, fulfilling and fun. I love what I do, and the best part of owning my firm is that I'm able to have the flexibility I need and want for my kids and our lifestyle.

The clients who come into my life are exactly the type I most want to work with. They're creative, kind, honest, smart and driven to succeed. My clients work with me as their marketing/ PR partner, and together we accomplish fantastic results for their businesses.

I'm able to use my gifts in ways that helps others. That seems to be a theme in my life that works well with my gifts.

APPLICATION

Your gifts from God are meant to be explored, recognized and used. You have many.

Trust and have faith in the desire you have within you. It's a map to discovering your gifts, and it's a beacon to success.

PRAYER

Dear God, thank you for helping me to recognize and use the wonderful gifts You have blessed me with. Please help me to continually discover my hidden talents and skills, and guide me as I follow the desires You place within me. Help me to have, and act on, the faith that Jesus taught. I ask this in Jesus' name. Amen.

DAILY DECLARATION

My gifts are from God, and I strive to recognize them and use them for the life I was created to live. #FaithIntoAbundance

MEET LISA AVEDON

Lisa Avedon is principal of IdeaWorks, a digital marketing/PR firm focused on helping companies boost their sales and brand image.

Lisa's sharp brand positioning insights enable clients to define, refine and align their brand with powerful digital marketing and PR to generate long-term revenue and growth.

CONTACT LISA

IdeaWorks

WEBSITE
IdeaWorksbmc.com

FACEBOOK
Facebook.com/lavedon

LINKEDIN
LinkedIn.com/in/LisaAvedon

TWITTER
@IDAWorks

INSTAGRAM
@IDAWorks

DAY 9

100 X LIFE

STEPHEN F. SKINNER

"Still other seed fell on fertile soil. The seed grew and produced a crop that was a hundred times as much as had been planted!"

Luke 8:8

Have you ever planted some really nice flowers that looked great at the nursery, but after about a week they were dying? That was me.

I am, by background, a pharmacist. Well, I am actually an entrepreneur trapped in a pharmacist's body. I have had a 20-year career as a compounding pharmacist, a pharmacy owner, and a health food store owner.

Although I did not start with a passion for natural medicine and the old-fashioned art of compounding, over the years it really grew. Like the Jimmy Buffett song about a pirate, I felt like a pharmacist 100 years too late! Pharmacy has been very good to me, and I feel blessed to have discovered these niches of the profession.

I have started, run, and successfully sold several businesses through the years, some of them in health care. I am now running two companies. One is a real-estate-development company. The other is a business- and life-coaching company, which involves speaking engagements and training, of which this book is a part.

The problem was that I had a lot of success right from the get-go in my career. I really thought it was all me. I thought that it came from my hard work. Indeed, some of it did. But what I was ignoring was the fact that I was given some gifts to be able to do the hard work, to pursue those ventures, and I was being blessed. Instead, I attributed my success only to *me*. I really thought that I was "Mr. Midas." Everything I was going to touch would turn to gold. And, in many cases, it did.

However, like King Midas of the fairy tale legend, this success came at great cost. I really ignored some things in my life. I ignored my children and my wife. I was working six days a week. I was working all the time, often eating all three meals at the pharmacy. I would leave before my kids woke up and return after they were asleep. I even missed a birthday party.

I took advantage of a lot of people, both my employees and my colleagues. I also ignored my health. I was eating whatever I could (often a hamburger), whenever I could, as fast as I could. I was stressed out at work and at home. I was working all the time, just grabbing things to eat really quickly. I was not sleeping well, so I was drinking Diet Cokes in order to get energy to get through the hectic day. I was finding that my teeth were hurting and I was grinding them at night.

Then all of a sudden, everything just caved in on me. Overnight, my pharmacy lost a major client. With that client went over a quarter of my profits. I was overweight. I had gotten some worrisome reports back from my doctor. My cholesterol was high and my blood sugar was erratic. I was only in my early thirties, but I was overweight, and increasingly bad-tempered.

I started losing people around me. I started losing staff members. I just thought that people were disposable and they were there to serve me. Somebody might have looked at me and thought I had it all, that I was very successful. On the outside I was, but on the inside I was miserable.

THE LESSON OF FAITH

I finally came to the realization that all of this was happening because God was reaching out to me. He was telling me, "Stephen, you think you did all this, but you didn't do *any* of this. I gave these things to you and if you don't change some of your ways, I may just take it all away." It became a very lonely, very dark time in my life.

I really didn't know what to do. I had reached a point where I was going to start drinking heavily or do something even worse. At the same time, my father was starting to experience a lot of health problems, including rheumatoid arthritis, arteriosclerosis, and colon cancer, all within a few months. The image of him on the table with tubes going everywhere stuck with me. I remembered how much I despised hospitals. Although hospitals and those who work in them do an incredible service, hospitals give me the creeps, and they are depressing to me.

I am extremely thankful my wife stuck with me. I put her through incredible difficulty because of the way I was living. I must frankly state that she is an incredible woman, the most selfless person I know. I tell people *she* is the reason we are still married, 20 years at the time of this writing. It's not because of me!

But even with her patience, I was still in a terrible state. The anxieties over money, work, and my father's failing health, compounded by my neglect of my wife and our children—all of this was destroying me from the inside. The physical abuse I gave myself—bad diet, no exercise, long hours of nothing *but* work—these were destroying me from the outside. I was losing myself and everything that meant anything at all.

That's when the transformation slowly began. God finds any way He can to help us, and my turnaround started in a very quiet way.

We had a dog named Jake. He was a little mutt and he always wanted to go for a walk. I started taking him out on a walk in the mornings. I started walking. I didn't really know what else to do. It was the only time I had for myself. I was so stressed out throughout my day. I was *still* working 12-hour days and eating all my meals at work, and each day I would come home to a very active house with a young daughter and twins! So I started getting up early and walking Jake, while listening to an iPod.

I started searching for anything positive I could find to listen to. I listened to positive music. I started to listen to different podcasts, like Joel Osteen's, John Maxwell's, and anything else I could find that was something positive. I didn't want to hear anything negative.

INTO ABUNDANCE

And even from this bare beginning, changes began to take place. I began to notice the incredible beauty of the sunrise, and how it was different each day. Over time, that morning walk became an oasis of refreshment for me.

Eventually my dog passed away, but the seeds of change had been sown. I eventually moved from walking to intense exercise, really devoting the first couple of hours of my mornings to my spirit and body. People who knew me started to ask, "What's changed about you? You're looking better; you aren't as negative as you were."

Now I'm in the best shape of my life. My health is great. I sleep well. I have peace. I've got tons of joy that I just want to share with other people. I'm now living with intention. I have a purpose. I tell people I'm now fueled by *supernatural* and *natural power*. I've discovered that *this is the best way to live!*

God also changed how I look at work. I now look at business as a ministry. I ask Him who I can serve each day, and to use me to make a difference for Him. On top of that, I am getting incredible results. In the past year, I have been able to do the following:

- Written 5 books, one of which became a best seller in Christian Professional Growth.

- Launched a podcast with 50 episodes and over 100,000 downloads.

- Participated in a groundbreaking project called *The 17 Biblical Principles of Success*

- Successfully completed two real estate development projects.

- Spoken at several large corporate and faith based events.

- Coached other business owners on how to create their excellent life, and build a great business.

- Gone on a 12-day mission trip.

- Helped coach my son's football team.

- Traveled all over the country with my family on vacations.

- Been at home for dinner way more than I ever used to.

APPLICATION

This system evolved into a daily morning routine anyone can stick to. I call it *The 100X Life System*. It is based on the scripture above, and it is designed to help make your soil fertile so it can produce as much as 100X!

These are 7 simple daily habits that anyone with a smartphone, and a pair of shoes, can do. I use an acronym to help remember them called PLANT.

Every day I will:

> **P**ray & Praise (To God)
> **L**isten & Learn (From God first, then others)
> **A**ct (Take Action-Respond to God's promptings, Exercise,
> Make a To Do List)
> **N**ourish (My Spirit, Mind & My Body)
> **T**hankful (Have Gratitude)

These habits create a fertile soil that produces FRUIT.

> **F**reedom!
> **R**esults!
> **U**nity!
> **I**mpact!
> **T**ransformation!

Try the system and see for yourself. You will get incredible results in your life. Your focus, your energy, your mental clarity, and your way of dealing with other people will all improve. Most importantly, the fruits of this are the very best offered anyone at any time.

Consider this list, found in Galatians 5:22-23, and called the Fruit of the Holy Spirit: love, joy, peace, patience, kindness, goodness, faithfulness, gentleness, and self-control. I have found a way to experience all these in my life, and you can as well!

PRAYER

Father, we have a short time here on earth to make a difference. We have a race to run. There's a lot counting on us. The people around us need us. We're no good to anyone if we're sick all the time, if we're not living to be the masterpiece you created us to be. We can't be used for all that you want to use you for if we're overwhelmed, if we're stressed, if we're preoccupied, or dealing with poor health, a rotten attitude, and a despairing state of mind. We acknowledge that many of our health issues, our bad habits, and our addictions are from the enemy attacking our weaknesses. But where we are weak, YOU ARE STRONG! Your son has defeated the enemy, so we stand not in fear, but in the power of your son Jesus, our savior. We ask you to heal us in His name, Amen."

DAILY DECLARATION

I'm now fueled by supernatural and natural power. I've discovered that this is the best way to live! #FaithIntoAbundance

MEET STEPHEN F. SKINNER

Stephen F. Skinner is a Speaker, Business Coach, Entrepreneur, as well as a licensed Pharmacist.

He's the author of a #1 Bestseller in Christian Professional Growth & Personal Transformation – '*The 100X LIFE: 7 Simple Daily Habits That Will Transform Your Life, Unlock Your Greatest Potential, and Create a Life Beyond Your Wildest Dreams*'.

He's started, run, and successfully sold several businesses in his 20-year entrepreneurial career, mostly in health care and wellness.

Today, many people consider him *"The Go-To Facilitator of Faith Based Peer-to-Peer Groups supporting Christian Male Entrepreneurs & Small Business Owners in the Southeast"*

CONTACT STEPHEN

WEBSITE
StephenFSkinner.com

FACEBOOK
Facebook.com/SkinnerConsultingLLC

TWITTER
@StephenFSkinner

LINKEDIN
LinkedIn.com/in/StephenFSkinner

THE $50 MILLION MAN THAT BECAME HOMELESS

JAIME SMITH

"For I consider that the sufferings of this present time are not worth comparing with the glory that is to be revealed to us."

Romans 8:18

It wasn't one dynamic moment, but the culmination of a three-year downward spiral from what most people would have thought was the pinnacle of professional success.

I was using prescription medication to both help me stay productive at work during the day, and another medication to go to sleep at night. Eventually, I reached a point where I could not find enough of the medication I was taking to satisfy the physical habit that I had developed.

That was when I graduated from prescription drugs to using methamphetamine. I quickly went from just using meth, to absolutely everything I could find. I ended up being fully, 100% addicted to heroin and methamphetamine. I lost my businesses, my wealth, my investment properties, my family, every single one of my friends, all my possessions, all my assets, custody of my daughter, and my freedom.

I was so angry with God. I thought, "There is no reason that God would put someone through this much loneliness, hopelessness, and physical and emotional pain."

I didn't have a place to live, I had zero money and I had no resources. I literally had gone from having a $50 million a year business, driving a Lamborghini, and living in a million-dollar mansion to being homeless, staying in a shelter and riding the bus.

The first job I was able to get was on a family farm shoveling cow manure. That family had me start writing a list. They said, "Jamie, write a list of every God-inspired action, every Godly intervention, and every divine intervention that happens."

All of a sudden, I had a list where there was six, then seven, then eight, then nine, then ten things. I literally fell to my knees and said, "That's it. I cannot do this without you, I cannot do this without you."

From that point forward, from the time I brought God back in my life, it has just been one blessing after another, after another, after another.

THE LESSON OF FAITH

The lesson I learned is that no matter how dark, hopeless, or negative, a situation is we have to trust that God is putting us through these things for the greater good.

There's always a greater good that happens from an action. Think of your life as a woman giving birth. Your life is in this really nice comfortable place. It's warm, it's cozy, you're fed, and you're totally taken care of. Then all of a sudden you're not. It's cold, noisy and some guy hangs you upside down and slaps your bottom. But what seems to be a negative situation is actually just the beginning of something far greater.

INTO ABUNDANCE

My life and my businesses are so much more stress free, because when a challenge comes up I hand it over to God.

I really allow God to guide me in making the most accurate decision. When I do that, things always work out. If a situation doesn't work out for a certain reason, I have to find the lesson and find the opportunity in it.

My destination now was not to regain my life, but to transform it. I mended relationships, embraced my daughter with a consuming love that would never again be tried. I leaned on my faith and recognized that His motivation became my mission.

From the depth of this journey my companies under the Alchemy umbrella were born. Alchemy is to find the power in the process of transforming something common into something special. Alchemy is about creating a new legend of elements where lives are not only restored, but are transformed.

APPLICATION

Hand any difficult decisions over to God, and do the right thing because the right thing will always reap the best rewards. If you do the right thing and one hundred percent of your actions are correct and in line with what God would want, the best situation will come of it.

PRAYER

Help my soul find rest in you God; my salvation only comes from you.

DAILY DECLARATION

Live your Legend. #FaithIntoAbundance

MEET JAIME SMITH

Jaime's story is of a man who had everything and eventually found himself in the cold embrace of prison.

As the author of his destiny it was in these moments, these dark foreboding caverns of pain that a spark of light pierced his soul. The reflection on his existence, the ache, the loss, and the devastation would not be his legacy; it would simply be his lesson.

With a hunger lit inside his very being, the fire of ambition that was once his downfall began to flame brighter. The destination now was not to regain his life, but to transform his life.

With fight and desire in his spirit he began climb. He mended his relationships and he embraced his daughter with a consuming love that would never again be tried. He was humbled and walked in grace. He leaned on his faith and recognized that his motivation became his mission.

From the depth of this journey Alchemy was born. Alchemy is to find the power in the process of transforming something common into something special. Alchemy is about creating a new legend of elements where lives are not only restored, but are transformed.

CONTACT JAIME

Alchemy Holdings, Alchemy Apparel

FACEBOOK
Facebook.com/Jaime.Smith.hub

LINKEDIN
LinkedIn.com/in/JaimeAlexanderSmith

DAY 11

I'M NOT GOING TO DIE TODAY

CYDNEY BULGER, ESQ.

"The righteous person may have many troubles, but the LORD delivers him from them all."

Psalms 34:19

I looked into my rearview mirror, and I saw a truck coming at me very fast. There was absolutely no way they were going to stop. I started to panic. I was in traffic so I couldn't move. I couldn't get out. There was nothing I could do.

They hit me.

After the initial impact, I sat there and began to gather myself. I was okay; nothing was broken. I was alive.

Then, another car hit me and another and another. At that point, my car was spinning 360 degrees on the highway, and all I could think was "God, please be here. Be here right now."

I like to listen to the Christian radio station on my way to work because it keeps me calm driving in traffic. At the time of the accident, there was a particular song playing called "God, I Need You," and that was the only thing that I could hear. I couldn't hear the blast. I couldn't hear the crashing. I couldn't hear brakes. Nothing. All I could hear was that music.

At that point, I knew. I was terrified, but I knew. I thought, "I'm not going to die. God's not going to let me die today. Not going to happen."

I was certainly injured, but not grievously so. That was the moment where God said, "Hey, I'm here, and I'm with you. I'm not going to leave you."

Ever since then, it changed the way that I see the world.

THE LESSON OF FAITH

Even if the circumstances around you are physically terrifying, and you don't see it, God is there. He is with you.

I think the most important thing the accident showed me is the absolute lack of control that we have over really anything in this life. All you can do is let go and allow God to work through whatever circumstance you are in.

INTO ABUNDANCE

The lack of control in that event really stuck with me. Since I've been in business for myself, there are times where things are booming, and it's great. I try to look at what is going on and say, "Okay, what am I doing right? What can I continue to do?"

There have been times when things are not as busy, and it's difficult to stay away from doubt and stay away from getting nervous. I always remember that I can work hard, apply what I've learned, and do everything right, but at the end of the day I am not in control of any of this.

That gives me a lot of peace, actually, because I'm not in charge anyhow, so I can only do my best and trust that God is going to handle the rest of it, which he always does.

APPLICATION

I think most entrepreneurs want to be in charge and want to be in control of things. It's only natural.

As an entrepreneur, you are in control of pretty much every aspect of your business, but you should be mindful that you are ultimately not the person in charge. Whatever plan you do have, maybe it aligns with God's plan, maybe it doesn't. Always keep an eye to what He's trying to do in your life, that He's trying to do with your business and serve that first. I think that gives the best reward.

PRAYER

God, please go before me in all that I do and make the crooked places straight. I know that by your strength I can do all things, and without it, I can do nothing. I have nothing but that which you have given me, and I thank you for all that I have. Please give me your grace and guidance in all that I do. In your holy name I pray, Amen"

DAILY DECLARATION

You will never be too important to be kind #FaithIntoAbundance

MEET CYDNEY BULGER, ESQ.

Cydney Bulger is a graduate of the University of Georgia and Florida Coastal School of Law.

Cydney started her career as an attorney for the State of Florida, prosecuting cases of child abuse and neglect. Cydney then entered private practice, where she worked exclusively in family law.

In 2015, she opened The Bulger Firm to provide clients with aggressive representation and excellent service.

CONTACT CYDNEY

The Bulger Firm, PLLC

WEBSITE
TheBulgerFirm.com

FACEBOOK
Facebook.com/TheBulgerFirm

LINKEDIN
LinkedIn.com/in/CydneyBulger

INSTAGRAM
@thebulgerfirm

DAY 12

MY EYES OF FAITH
WERE OPENED

JIM SCHNEIDER

"All things are working together for good in my life because I love God and I am called according to His purpose."

Romans 8:28

My most defining moment was at age 40. I was doing significantly well in the midst of the financial crisis that was happening in 2008-2009. Through the power of prayer, I was moved to resign my career, sell all my hard-earned assets, and start an eyewear company that honors God.

I went from advising people about how to reduce their risk by transferring it to the insurance company, to transferring my risk and starting this company with God as the focus. The way I saw it, the greatest risk was not taking the risk at all.

The funny thing about that decision is that all I knew about eyewear, I learned from my wife Amy, who is the brains behind the operation. She always did a beautiful job fitting me for glasses and was the only one of us who had optical experience.

I barely knew anything about the optical industry, nor did I know how to start a business. It was by the power of prayer, however, that God provided the purpose, passion, and the unyielding perseverance for me to be successful.

THE LESSON OF FAITH

God will never lead you into something that is too easy. He wants to give you purpose, and for that to happen, you must glorify and rely on Him. That is the lesson I received.

There were so many times when I said to myself, "I just can't do this. I don't have what it takes." If that perseverance factor ever fades, God will always put people in your path for encouragement. It could be your spouse, or it could be somebody else.

However, you've got to accept that the path will not always be easy. There will be challenges.

God's plan may not necessarily be your plan. God wants you to lean on him. He wants you to be patient. We are all going to make mistakes, but we must make an effort to learn from those mistakes, grow in our wisdom, and become more Christ-like.

When I look at the visible (pun intended) lessons of my business, it is not making impetuous decisions. If we have a tough decision we have to make, my wife and I always use the phrase 'stop, drop, and pray.' We have to ask God for guidance every single day. We must make an effort to make sure we do not make the same mistake twice.

INTO ABUNDANCE

God has shown me that abundance arrives in far better things than money and objects. If we didn't start Eyes of Faith, so many wonderful blessings would have never happened: traveling to amazing places like Kenya to give the gift of sight and help spread the word of God; building wonderful relationships with hundreds of people that I would have never met; routinely traveling to beautiful locations in the US; spreading the word of God by preaching the gospel to thousands of open-minded people; being a conduit for mission work and fostering closeness to God; supporting Sight Ministries International and many other faith-based nonprofits that provide the gift of sight; as always, praying with people around the world that normally would not have a praying opportunity.

APPLICATION

One of my favorite questions to ask when I'm sensing reluctance from aspiring entrepreneurs is, "What is holding you back?"

I tell them to ask themselves that question and then pray for God to give them the plan and purpose to move forward.

Once God reveals that purpose, if there are still reservations, let God know. Tell God what is holding you back and let Him bestow guidance and wisdom upon you so that you may persevere and receive your blessing.

PRAYER

Dear Lord, I pray that Your guiding thoughts will stir the passion in every reader of this book to take on Your purpose for their life. We know the world may consider Your purpose for them too risky, but there is no risk in following You. Thank you for loving us and leading us. We love You...In the name of Jesus, I pray.

DAILY DECLARATION

What is holding you back? Your biggest risk could be not taking the risk at all. #FaithIntoAbundance

MEET JIM SCHNEIDER

Jim honed sales, contract negotiation, and relationship management skills during eight years at The Cincinnati Financial Corporation as an Insurance Underwriter and Territory Manager presiding over northeastern Ohio and northwestern Pennsylvania. Jim managed 30 independent agencies with a focus on new business development and field underwriting of commercial insurance, representing millions in premium volume.

Following his tenure at Cincinnati Financial, Jim accepted a position with a Cincinnati agency working directly with Gilbert's Risk Solutions in Sharon, Pennsylvania. As a Commercial Risk Manager for Gilbert's, Jim cultivated a zero revenue segment of commercial business to a multi-million dollar portfolio.

Since founding Eyes of Faith Optical in 2008, Jim has turned a fledgling eyewear company into a major niche in the optical industry.

Eyes of Faith is recognized not only as a leader in style and innovation but also as a philanthropic company that has been able to reach into some of the world's darkest corners with their Wear & Share® program. Through Wear & Share®, Eyes of Faith delivers the values of Christian faith through vision-specific mission work here and all over the world.

Jim has been profiled in many publications including a cover story about leadership in Vision Monday magazine and a feature article in Ministry Today magazine, plus numerous speaking engagements and radio interviews to inspire others with the Eyes of Faith story.

Jim is a graduate of Ohio Northern University and lives in West Middlesex, Pennsylvania with his wife, Amy, and daughter, Claire.

CONTACT JIM

Eyes of Faith Optical

WEBSITE
EOFOptical.com

FACEBOOK
Facebook.com/Eyes.of.Faith

TWITTER
@EyesofFaith

INSTAGRAM
@eyesoffaith1

DAY 13

THE MIRACLE AT THE US ATTORNEY'S OFFICE

DEMITRUS EVANS

> *"The Lord is good to those who wait hopefully and expectantly for Him, to those who seek Him [inquire of and for Him and require Him by right of necessity and on the authority of God's word]."*
>
> *Lamentations 3:25*

As a lawyer, I was on one of the biggest cases that I ever had, and it was in the Federal Court. While we were preparing for trial, some additional discovery was released. Some of the information was classified, so I had to go to the US Attorney's Office to go through this material.

As I was going through these boxes, there were two pages of scriptures in the midst of all of these documents and it didn't make sense to me. I sat there and read them. I knew that it was important for me to have those scriptures for this trial. I sandwiched the scriptures in between the other documents I needed.

I thought about how it was going to look to the US Attorneys on the other side when they got it. Exactly what I expected to happen, happened. As they were going through it and making copies they asked, "Why do you need this?"

I replied, "Well, this is part of what was recovered, and these are one of the things that I never had, so I don't know what it matches up to," which was truthful.

When I got back to my office, I prayed and asked, "God, what is this about?"

He said, "I am giving you the strategy."

There were about seven other lawyers on the same case, and so true enough, the other lawyers took almost every piece of it and in the scriptures, it said, "You have to pray and then you will see my salvation."

God had just laid it in my lap. I recognized that God sometimes hides things from us. If I had received that very early in the case, I have no idea what I would have done with it. It would not have meant nearly what it meant to me after that. It was at a time when things in the case had gotten tough.

I said, "Father, I don't see how I am supposed to win this. I don't understand where you are in this. Help."

When I got it, I realized that I don't always know, but he knew. His timing was already perfect, and that was already there before I was even a lawyer on the case. It's not like God had an angel in the US Attorney's Office and put it there. The scriptures were already there for me.

THE LESSON OF FAITH

I learned that God is not always going to give you all the answers, the strategy, the clear vision. You have to trust because sometimes He is just going to give you piece by piece.

He may give it to you when it's the hardest, and when you are trying to say, "I don't see you, father. Where are you?" It may be according to your needs, or how much you need it. I was at the point where I thought, "I have to hear from you right now, please or this is not going to work," but then the timing was right and God, he already put the ram in the bush.

INTO ABUNDANCE

I started this business six years ago. I pray about everything in the business, and I do that with my staff and with cases. I have come to realize that God has his own plan and strategy for certain cases, and I should just let God take the wheel as He steers me onto the right path.

One of the ways I have applied God into my company is by praying, asking him for guidance each and every day. When I feel like I've reached a wall he has always been there to guide me around it.

I just trust that if I don't know something, He is going to provide it, and He always has. God is always there when you need him the most.

APPLICATION

Being able to use scripture in business is key. I've heard just phenomenal stories about Christian business owners who pray every day and ask for this strategy, pray for their business plans and just pray for God to really get involved from the beginning.

The scriptures I found that day have been the most powerful for me. I was praying, looking for the strategy, but then I realized, the scriptures were my strategy! I put them up, and it was clear that the mission of the company and the values this company is founded upon, come from those scriptures.

PRAYER

Thank you God for going before me and making the crooked paths straight, for protecting me and my family and allowing me to be a blessing to the world and point them towards you. In Jesus' name.

DAILY DECLARATION

Expect only great things to happen today because of the favor shield and keys that He has given. #FaithIntoAbundance

MEET DEMITRUS EVANS

Attorney Demitrus Evans earned her J.D. from the University of Miami School of Law in Florida in 1994 where she worked on Asylum applications. She was admitted to the Illinois Bar in 1997, The Illinois Appellate Court Bar in 1998, the Federal District Court Trial Bar, The United States Supreme Court, The Federal Circuit and the International Court of Trade from 2000-2001.

Beginning her law career with Amnesty International in Chicago in 1998, she matriculated to the Federal Appellate Defenders Office, then held a clerkship with The Law Office of Ted Stein, in employment discrimination, and landed her first associate position with Ron Samuel & Associates, a general law practice in the Chicago Loop practicing civil, corporate, and contractual and employment discrimination. Her Civil Rights training was honed at The Law Office of Standish E. Willis where she prosecuted 1983 violations and defended high-level Federal criminal conspiracy and fraud cases as a Federal Defender Panel Attorney. She would later use these skills to serve as Bar Attorney through the Cook County Bar Association's Combined Bar Program and start a Nonprofit to help the innocent, TEEP (The Evans Exoneration Project).

Her corporate work took an international turn at the National Railway Company where she prosecuted trademarks and worked on international sales and distributorships. This work has continued at TEIL Firms LLC, where she manages a team of five with an array of national and international interns. Her current caseload includes a corporate transactional work and litigation in the federal and state courts. She additionally arbitrates for the County of Cook Mandatory Arbitration Program deciding personal injury matters. In her spare time, she teaches two legal classes for the Joseph School of Business, holds local and national membership and positions in various organizations and is a Library Trustee for the Village of Westchester. Attorney Evans uses her faith in all that she does, but mostly as a mother of two girls, wife, marathoner, and believer in justice for all.

CONTACT DEMITRUS

The Evans International Law Firms, LLC

WEBSITE

Teilfirms.com/teil-media-1

LINKEDIN

LinkedIn.com/in/DemitrusEvans

FACEBOOK

Facebook.com/The-Evans-International-Law-Firms-TEIL-Firms-LLC-280927988703667/

DAY 14

HOW $14 CHANGED MY LIFE

MALCOLM X. ADAMS

"He who gives to the poor will never want, but he who shuts his eyes will have many curses."

Proverbs 28:27

One day, shortly after turning 18, a family standing in front of me in line at the pharmacy became very upset. I could tell by the look in the father's eyes that he was in excruciating pain and in dire need of his prescription.

The cost for his prescription was only fourteen dollars, but it was fourteen dollars that he did not have. I decided to help out by walking around and asking people to donate. I must have walked a total of five miles before I collected the money to cover this man's prescription.

When I got back, the family was still standing in front of the store. I gave them the money and they got back in line and picked up the prescription. We talked for maybe twenty to thirty minutes, and within the span of our conversation, I could tell that the medication had done its job and alleviated the man's pain.

I will never forget how grateful those people were to me, a complete stranger.

THE LESSON OF FAITH

This particular occurrence taught me a few lessons simultaneously, most notably that it is not what the package looks like that matters but the gift inside that does.

I also learned that I should always strive to be a humble and cheerful giver and that I should keep in mind that most situations are bigger than myself. I believe the less a person makes it about themselves, the more of a part of the big picture they become.

INTO ABUNDANCE

It reinforced my belief that we brothers and sisters in Christ should always be willing to add value to other people's lives, both personally and in a business setting as well. When we see someone in pain, we should at least attempt to provide a fix, no matter what the problem is.

So, I do as many favors as possible, particularly for those that do not have much money. I believe that by doing favors, you end up being favored.

APPLICATION

My fellow Christian entrepreneurs can apply this lesson to their businesses by personifying the belief that we should be of service to others because it is the right thing to do, not because of the potential profit we could make might make from doing so. A lot of my business comes from that ideology.

The more active I am in the community, or just in the ministry of helping other people, the more business I end up with. It goes hand in hand. According to the law of reciprocity, you have to give to receive. Taking ten percent of quarterly earnings and doing a food drive for the homeless, or making sure kids have school supplies when it's time to return to school, are perfect examples of selfless acts that will bring us blessings and rewards from God.

PRAYER

Father I thank you. I thank you for this mind. Thank you for this body. Thank you for this spirit. Thank you. Thank you. Thank you God.

DAILY DECLARATION

If the outcome, isn't income; it's a waste of time, thought and energy. #FaithIntoAbundance

MEET MALCOLM X. ADAMS

Jetset Consulting, L.L.C. is a brainchild of the tech-renaissance. Like many people in this Age of Information, our knowledge base is broad. What distinguishes us, however, from the rank and file is the corresponding depth of that knowledge. In addition to knowing "a lot about a lot," we are capable of synthesizing ideas into the most effective real-world solution to any given challenge. Just as the founder of Jetset Consulting L.L.C., we are facilitators of both ideas and action. This synergy of theory and praxis exemplifies the holistic paradigm that is increasingly necessary in the modern business environment.

Jetset Consulting L.L.C. is a full-service IT consulting and services provider and the principles of its founder permeate our business environment and practices.

Information Technology is playing a larger role in our lives, and working people are choosing to provide themselves with superior productivity and greater efficiency. Loving families with active children and an interactive learning environment require better service providers to ensure the success of their children and peace of mind for themselves. Busy tech lovers are flocking to an ever-growing number of retail sellers and "break-fix" facilities across the nation to conform to the standards of quality set by a rapidly developing industry. To meet these ever-evolving needs, we at Jetset Consulting develop relationships instead of selling commodities.

CONTACT MALCOLM

Jetset Consulting, LLC

WEBSITE
JetSetitc.com

FACEBOOK
Facebook.com/JetsetConsultingLLC/

TWITTER
@jetsetinfo

LINKEDIN
LinkedIn.com/in/Malcolm-Adams-65559990

INSTAGRAM
@jetsetinfo

DAY 15

NOW I GET CALLED?
REALLY, GOD?!?!

LISA ASHE, D.O.

"Trust in the Lord with all your heart. Never rely on what you think you know. Remember the Lord in everything you do, and he will show you the right way."

Proverbs 3:5,6

Medical school was the biggest moment in my life and brought me closer to God. It was both a blessing and a burden, as it was the first time in my life where I experienced failure.

School had always been an easy process, but when I got to medical school, it was a huge awakening for me. I had to relearn how to study, and how to deal with not always getting a 98% on my tests. It was a big shock for me, but I learned more from the failures and mistakes than from what I actually got right.

It also produced a certain amount of humility, and so I'm grateful for that time. I don't take the blessing lightly because we really had to work hard for it. God gave me more than I asked for.

I grew up in my parents' church, but when I got to medical school, I began attending the church around the corner from the school. It was the first time I chose my own church, and I was excited to go all the time. It brought me closer to God, and that increased my relationship with Him.

My call to ministry came about three weeks before I graduated from medical school. I didn't know quite what to do with it because I was graduating. The pastor at the church reminded me that Luke was a physician, and that I would be able to do both. I am doing both now, so I think the struggle and success of med school is definitely what changed me.

THE LESSON OF FAITH

When God directs us or gives us a vision, a goal, or a promise in our lives, it's not always as simple as one plus one equals two.

The Israelites show us that in the wilderness sometimes the process has detours and other stops along the way. Some of those detours come with mistakes and failures, but that doesn't mean that it's not all a part of God's plan and what he promised you is not still going to come to fruition.

You have to be prayerful as well as persistent. Be prayerful because you have to have discernment and direction from God; be persistent because oftentimes our promise requires our participation.

INTO ABUNDANCE

When starting your own business, you learn what works and what doesn't work. I put a lot of money into marketing strategies in the beginning that didn't pan out.

It was tough at the time, but I learned that it was okay if the marketing plan didn't succeed at first. It just meant I simply needed to change marketing strategies. Now, I'm very prayerful and discerning about which direction I market the business. I think that persistence, prayer and your prayer life should be number one for entrepreneurs.

If I don't get as many patients as I projected, or make as much money as I projected one month, I don't get upset about it. I don't consider it a complete failure. It's just a setback. It doesn't mean that the business is not going to work, or that I followed God's vision wrong.

APPLICATION

The first thing entrepreneurs should be prayerful about is choosing what type of business they are going to start, and how they're going to do it.

The second is being persistent. Once you get the vision, write it down. That is going to turn into your business plan. You have to be persistent in following that plan from there.

The third thing is to remember the vision that God gave you, and what you started out to do. In medical school, when you get to the second year, or even sometimes in the third year, there's a point where every medical student feels like they want to give up and they don't want to do it anymore. You have to go back to that vision, and see it to completion.

PRAYER

God, thank you for being who you are. Thank you for allowing me to have a relationship with you. Guide me, keep me, and make your will for my life plain that I may live out your purpose on purpose. Thank you for everything God.

DAILY DECLARATION

When God says "yes", no one else can say "no".
#FaithIntoAbundance

MEET DR. LISA ASHE

Dr. Lisa Ashe serves as the Medical Director of Be Well Medical Group, a leading concierge medicine and wellness group currently serving the Washington D.C., Maryland, and Virginia metro areas. A Board Certified Internal Medicine physician, Dr. Lisa has completed countless certifications and training programs throughout the United States and abroad. She is a member of the American Medical

Association, American Osteopathic Association and the American College of Physicians.

Before founding Be Well Medical Group, Dr. Lisa was the Medical Director at Doctors Community Hospital, where she was responsible for the daily activities of the Clinical Decision and Observation Units.

Dr. Lisa completed her residency at George Washington University and Providence Hospital in Washington, D.C., and her internship at Georgetown University. Dr. Lisa earned her medical degree at the Philadelphia College of Osteopathic Medicine.

She also received her Masters of Divinity from the Samuel Dewitt Proctor School of Theology at Virginia Union University. She was licensed to preach in 2014 at the Alfred Street Baptist Church in Alexandria, Virginia.

She has received numerous awards, including the National Congress of Black Women's Shirley Chisholm Award, Adam Clayton Powell Scholarship, Skinner Leadership Institute, and was awarded the key to the city of Camden, NJ.

CONTACT LISA

Be Well Medical Group

WEBSITE
BeWellMedicine.com

FACEBOOK
Facebook.com/Be-Well-Medical-Group-1118445898183884/

INSTAGRAM
@bewellmed

TWITTER
@bewellmed

PLAN FOR GROWTH

DAVID D. SIMONS

> *"Now to Him who is able to [carry out His purpose and] do superabundantly more than all that we dare ask or think [infinitely beyond our greatest prayers, hopes, or dreams], according to His power that is at work within us, to Him be the glory in the church and in Christ Jesus throughout all generations forever and ever. Amen."*
>
> *Ephesians 3:20-21*

I have learned that life will throw different obstacles, but you must always plan your life and the growth you want to experience no matter what comes your way. My wife and I were on vacation in Bakersfield, CA visiting my family for Christmas.

We had a great time and enjoyed our stay but at the same time, I was going through one of the most challenging seasons of my life professionally. I worked full time for a green company overseeing the social media marketing and strategy for the company. At the same time, I was running my digital media agency. About three months earlier, a mentor and good friend of mine introduced me to his mastermind of automotive clients. After a presentation, half of them signed up for my social media services on a monthly retainer.

While my mother and my wife were cooking all the goodies we were planning to eat, I spent half of my Christmas day catching up on work for my job and my clients.

So here I was at Christmas doing my best to be a family man and manage my 9-to-5, and run my business at the same time. I was overwhelmed with all the work I had to do. My family could noticeably tell that I was stressed and distracted, but soon after our vacation, my entire world changed.

On January 6th, I got to work and could tell something was different, I could feel it in the atmosphere. As I was speaking to my boss, I noticed he wasn't as cheery as normal.

That same day, one of the ladies overseeing the marketing department asked me to do a project for her. She said, "David I have this project directly from the CEO, and it needs to be completed by Friday."

I said, "Yes indeed, I will get it done." At first, I thought it was strange that the CEO asked me to do a project directly, especially since he never asked me to do that before.

The project itself was strange as well. I was being asked to create a training document for everything I do and all the different elements that I use to train the 22 countries that I managed.

I persisted in working on it in addition to handling all the work that piled up after my vacation. I worked on it from Wednesday to Friday and not too long after hitting the send button, my boss asked to speak to me.

This Friday already felt a little strange, but when I saw my boss walk into the room with the HR representative, I knew something was up.

My boss had an uneasy look on his face, and he is usually a very fun-loving guy. With a sense of urgency, he said, "David I don't know any other way to put this, but you have been terminated."

At that moment my heart sank, and I was in shock and disbelief. I didn't even know what to say at first, but after I managed to get a control of my tongue, I said, "Ok, was there something I did that caused this?"

My boss told me a few things that the executive team said. The reasons weren't very compelling reasons for firing someone, especially since there weren't any warnings.

I was directed to pack my personal belongings because that was going to be my last day. After packing, I had a very long train ride home. I thought about how unexpected this was and how I felt embarrassed, disappointed, thrilled, and anxious all at the same time.

I was very worried about what I would say to my wife, but one thing I was not worried about was my occupation.

Back in December, I was on a coaching call and my coach said to me, "David, you need to quit your job and go into business full time. That is the only way you're going to be able to achieve your dreams. Your job is weighing you down."

I told him, "You are crazy. There is no way I am doing that right now."

However, after fighting with the thought of leaving my job, I spoke to my wife and told her what I was thinking.

She said, "Sweetie, I am in agreement with you leaving your job and going into full-time entrepreneurship."

You need to understand something; my wife doesn't just say stuff like that because she is a very safe person and would choose safety over risk. As soon as she told me yes, I knew that God was at work. Soon after that, my coach and I set the launch date for me to leave my job.

Back in December, I told him I want to leave February 29th, and I put that on my calendar. My job let me go on January 8th, which is way sooner than I expected. I planned on leaving, but I did not plan on leaving that soon or in that fashion.

However, on my train ride home on that dark Friday evening, I remember waiting for my wife to come pick me up. I was shouting as loud as I could praising God for how great He is. It had always been my dream to be a full-time entrepreneur. In fact, before I even started my job at my former company, I was already running my business part time and had a few clients.

The other crazy thing about it is that I had read a book titled, "Caught Between A Dream and A Job" by Delatorro McNeal, a world renowned speaker and peak performance expert.

The book taught that to achieve your dreams, you should find your dream job then transition into your dream because most people waste their time on jobs that do not relate to their dreams at all.

I originally planned to leave my dream job as the Global Digital Media Manager after two years, but it ended up taking four years instead.

So now that I had been let go, I still had a business to run and clients to serve and a week later, my biggest client canceled on me.

Here I was recently laid off and had also lost my biggest client. I was at my breaking point and I was completely distraught. I then got into my prayer closet and asked for God to intervene with my mind because mentally I was in a whirlwind.

Two weeks later, my business partner and I signed a deal that was five times as much per month as the client that had just canceled.

THE LESSON OF FAITH

God is good, and He continues to blow my mind with all the amazing things He does for my family and me. Within this period, I had to get the revelation that GOD and GOD alone is my source. I always knew that my job was not my source, but I didn't understand that my business was not my source until I went through this process.

God wants us to rely on Him beyond anything and that means I can't even rely on my marketing genius to get clients. Just as much as I trust Him for salvation, I need to trust him to aid me in business.

INTO ABUNDANCE

Although God is there to help me in my business, I have an essential part to play and what I have realized is that God has given me the power of planning to map out my growth.

Most of us plan for emergencies, we plan for vacations, and we even plan for failure, but we never seem to plan for growth. God instructed me to plan for growth in my business before it started growing. He told me to build a team of people before I had the need for the team. I started looking for team members and interns before I had enough clients to justify it. It was soon after I had picked one of the social media managers for my team that my friend the automotive consultant introduced me to his clients.

My business grew when I planned for it to grow. You should do the same thing.

What would your business structure look like if you had a multi-million dollar business?

You don't need to guess. Plan for it!

APPLICATION

Write out a plan of the team you need to take your business to the next level. Write out all the functions you would need to have your business run like a well-oiled machine. Think big and expect big, do not minimize your business to a small operation, God is a BIG God and He doesn't think small. In fact, God has confined your success according to your thinking.

In Proverbs 23:7 it says, "As a man thinketh in his heart so is he...." Now take those thoughts and turn them into plans because one of the highest forms of faith is planning for what you want to happen.

PRAYER

Father God, I come before you today asking for you to enlarge my thinking and help me to see beyond myself so that I can use my business to help others and impact plenty of lives. Father, please help me to plan for growth because I know you will do abundantly above, beyond what I can ask, think or even imagine. Thank you, Father, in Jesus name Amen!

DAILY DECLARATION

Instead of planning for the worst I will plan for the best and expect the best because I serve the best God who has already given me His best, Jesus Christ. #FaithIntoAbundance

MEET DAVID D. SIMONS

David D. Simons is a mediapreneur who utilizes his off line and online skills to promote brands, increase businesses, support causes, and build relationships. His passion and excitement for media has attracted the likes of Fortune 500 companies, non-profits, churches, and entrepreneurs. David obtained a degree in Digital Media from Sacramento State University, and a Masters degree in Entertainment Business from Full Sail University. David is the CEO of Kingdom Social Media, which is an organization designed to teach business owners and business leaders how to effectively use social media to build their businesses. David has been recognized by Entrepreneur.com, Dell Computers, Yahoo, Xerox Corporation, and Hootsuite for his strategies in social media. David lives in

Philadelphia, PA with his loving wife, Abigail Simons. David lives by this rule: "The biggest risk you will take in life is not taking risks."

CONTACT DAVID

Kingdom Social Media

WEBSITE
KingdomSocialMedia.com

FACEBOOK
Facebook.com/KingdomSocialMedia

TWITTER
@DavidDSimons

LINKEDIN
LinkedIn.com/in/DavidDSimons

INSTAGRAM
@DavidDSimons

DAY 17

BACK TO POINT ZERO... AGAIN

JENNIFER XUE

> *"Come to me all you who are weary and burdened, and I will give you rest."*
>
> *Matthew 11:28*

I came to the United States with two pieces of luggage in pursuit of a graduate degree and freedom from persecution. I brought only a few months' worth of living expenses along with me. Being an optimist, I believed in my deepest heart that it wouldn't be that hard to find a job once I had settled in.

Quickly, I applied for a work permit with the Immigration and Naturalization Service (now US Citizenship and Immigration Services), which was available for persons from certain countries due to various hardships, including economic, religious, and political persecution. Indonesia, the country where I originated, was included.

Little did I know that God has something else in store for me. He wanted me to taste the hard life of being an international student and, eventually, a new immigrant. He wanted me to learn how to rely on Him than merely on my two bare hands.

After a few months of enjoying the busy life of a graduate student, my grandfather was diagnosed with colon cancer.

My mother was his only child, so she had to bear all the financial responsibilities that came with expensive cancer treatment. He didn't have health insurance because back then in Indonesia there was no government-managed healthcare and private health insurance was somewhat unheard of.

It hit me like a brick when I called home one day and she told me about the diagnosis and the cost of the treatment.

I couldn't concentrate on my studies and decided to drop out. I impatiently waited for the work permit to be issued, so I could start applying for jobs. I had to help my mom.

Then I started working odd jobs, such as making sushi, grooming dogs, and helping an attorney. But my contribution didn't last a long time as my grandfather lost his battle. The doctors said that his cancer had metastasized. I was completely heartbroken.

I had dropped out of school to work, and it didn't help much.

I was very close to my maternal grandparents as my biological father abandoned my mother and me before I was even born. I even called my grandmother "Mamma" and grandfather "Pappa" because they raised me. His passing broke my heart to pieces.

I continued working to support myself in this new land. There was an adage that said, "America is the land of opportunities." At that time, I was alone, poor, and grieving. I couldn't see where the opportunities were and began doubting many things.

I still worked in low-paying jobs and rented a cheap apartment. I was exhausted physically, mentally, and emotionally. I wanted to take a break, but I couldn't. I had to support myself.

Gradually, I applied for freelance writing jobs, as I wrote newspaper columns for several years before moving to the U.S. It was during the frenzy of Web 1.0, so I eventually worked for several dot-coms. My earning started to get better.

Alas, only slightly one year later, the dotcom bubble popped, and my income slid down with it. I was back to point zero again.

The exhaustion returned. I started to breathe in thick air, heard eery silence, and moved in slow motion. I felt the sadness of the whole world within while walking around with tons of brick on top of my head.

Looking back, I think I was in a depression. I didn't go to a physician or a therapist, as I thought it was a natural consequence after what I had gone through. And I didn't have any medical insurance.

[Disclaimer: If you are experiencing depression, it's recommended to visit a professional therapist or counselor, so you receive the most appropriate treatment. My experience may not be suitable for you, and this story is by no means a substitute for professional psychological and psychiatric therapies and counseling.]

I stayed in bed for weeks. After all, I didn't have a full-time job.

One day, when I had enough strength to move around, I went to a public library and found C.S. Lewis' *The Problem of Pain* and *A Grief Observed*. The titles fit my condition at that time.

They spoke volumes. Lewis wrote in *A Grief Observed*, "I thought I could describe a state; make a map of sorrow. Sorrow, however, turns out to be not a state but a process."

In *The Problem of Pain*, he wrote, "It is natural for us to wish that God had designed for us a less glorious and less arduous destiny, but then we wish not for more love but less."

Reading Lewis' books occupied my mind. His deep thoughts slowly awakened my zombie-like existence.

Since then, I've been living life to the fullest.

THE LESSON OF FAITH

When I felt that God had abandoned me and left me cold in a dark and dingy alley, He wanted me to rest.

Just like the footsteps in the sand poem, the pair of footsteps, I saw when I was depressed and grieving were not mine. They were His. He carried me on His back through the storm of life, while I was resting.

By experiencing hardships, He actually was training me to be a better self with a much bigger heart. Sorrows made me stronger, and hardships opened my heart for more love.

When you're tired and exhausted, take a rest.

INTO ABUNDANCE

The Lord woke me up from a zombie-like existence. Today, I'm living my fullest life understanding wholeheartedly that every bump on the road is merely a sign to slow down and take a rest.

From time to time, like in any business, my publishing and property investment businesses experience some cash flow problems. Instead of panicking, I now call such moments "resting periods."

I've gone through a lot in life, including multiple surgeries, deaths of loved ones, and a painful divorce. None defeated me. Instead, they made me stronger.

Low cash flow periods wouldn't defeat me. On the contrary, they are opportunities to reflect and rest for the next "battle." It's great timing to learn from mistakes and maintain my faith in God.

After all, He carried me during my darkest hours, why would He leave me this time around?

APPLICATION

Reflect upon your life. What were the moments when you doubted God's love for you? What did you do? What did He do?

While "everything happens for a reason" sounds like a cliché, it's actually not.

God wants us to experience life to the fullest, meaning we get to experience the good, the bad, and everything in between. He wants us to be better because of them. Because, through hardships, we are able to appreciate good things and love more.

And when the pain is too much, it's time for us to rest and heal.

PRAYER

"God, thank you for the good and the bad things in my life. They make me better and stronger person. Help me, Lord, whenever life is bad, to always remember that You're asking me to rest and heal so that I can be prepared for a better and stronger tomorrow. I trust my life in Your hands."

DAILY DECLARATION

Whenever things are bad, it's an opportunity to rest and heal. It's God's way to train me to be a better and stronger person. #FaithIntoAbundance

MEET JENNIFER XUE

Jennifer Xue is an award-winning author, columnist, and serial entrepreneur with proven record and strong dedication in gaining traction, brand awareness, and revenue generation. She is the founder of StyleCareer.com and SiliconValleyGlobe.com among other ventures. Her writing portfolio can be found at JenniferXue.com. When she's not writing, she plays with her dogs and travels the world.

CONTACT JENNIFER

WEBSITE
JenniferXue.com

FACEBOOK
Facebook.com/JenniferXueAuthor

LINKEDIN
LinkedIn.com/in/JenniferXue

TWITTER
@jenxuewrites

DAY 18

FROM DEATH COMES BIRTH

GARY LEBLANC

> *"Let us therefore come boldly unto the throne of grace, that we may obtain mercy, and find grace to help in time of need."*
>
> *Hebrews 4:16*

By this point, Brad's face resembled a skull rather than a face. It was late winter in 2012. His 3-year battle with lymphoma had gotten the better of him. He had days to live.

For years Brad underwent suffering that no human should endure. His routine consisted of chemotherapy, blood transfusions, and draining fluid from his lungs. I recall Brad often waking up in the middle of the night unable to breathe. This happened on a regular basis. And it happened even more frequently during an especially difficult round of chemo called DHAP.

Despite his dire circumstances, Brad always had hope. He needed to. His sister-in-law Elly and I made sure of that. We needed to convince Brad that there was a higher power at play and he would pull through.

Up until two days before he died, Brad felt he would beat cancer. I'll never forget that Saturday morning before he passed. All he said was, "I'm screwed."

Delirious from the morphine, this brief moment of clarity gave him the wherewithal to finally accept his fate. He had received a stem cell transplant just four weeks prior. It represented his last shot at a cure, but didn't go as planned. Brad took his final breath at 9:20 am, May 9, 2012. It was a Sunday morning. He was 45 years old.

I believe one's proximity to another's suffering has a commensurate impact. Brad's ordeal changed me. I had yet to learn exactly how much.

Near the end of Brad's life, I tried to make sense of his suffering. There are some questions that one cannot answer until they are near THE END. Brad and I would sit and talk about the "what ifs" in life. We would talk about how one's priorities change when the only desire in life is to be healthy. When what faces you is death, the only thing left to strive for is life.

At the time I was living a typical existence for a thirty-something year old young professional. I was Vice President for a Tier 1 company. My stresses consisted of where to shop on the weekend and how to make my life more exciting. Material took precedence over experiences. One could say I lived life at the surface. There was little depth, and hedonic pleasure took priority.

Under no uncertain terms, Brad would remind me how meaningless all that was. He gifted me the priceless perspective of a dying man – the perspective of someone facing their mortality head on.

During his ordeal, I had taken my coaching and personal training background to another level. Near the end of his life, I started to get my thoughts on paper. I leveraged my engineering and business degrees to deep-dive into holistic living. I was determined to engineer wellness. I strove to develop a guide to help the average person to avoid Brad's fate.

I quit my job in December of that year - seven months after Brad passed - and started my company Ikkuma. We published our first book, *Ikkuma: Evolution of Vitality,* less than a year after launch. The rest (as they say) is history.

THE LESSON OF FAITH

Upon becoming a Corporate Vice President, I would never have predicted this path that my life had taken. Brad's death catalyzed a transformation that was miraculous.

Living true to ourselves brings us closer to God. It brings us closer to that which brought us into the world. The more we deviate from our purpose, the further we stray from God; the further we stray from that divine energy that fuels our lives.

It took an enormous amount of suffering from a dear friend for my divine purpose to unearth itself. I find this eerily reminiscent to the suffering that Jesus incurred to right the wrongs of humanity. Sometimes it takes extreme sacrifice for people to truly see for the first time. Sometimes it takes extreme sacrifice to lift the fog of bad decisions and reveal our true purpose.

INTO ABUNDANCE

Brad's ordeal didn't just impact my business. That would be a gross understatement.

Brad's ordeal gave birth to my business. From his death was born a business whose belief is that every human has a best version of themselves. Ikkuma strives to help everyone find this optimal potential. We call it our "SuperHuman."

My life, my business, my future, would not exist had I not experienced the epitome of suffering through another soul. When you witness how little one has when they are at death's door, how can you not feel that your life has unlimited abundance?

Maintaining a scarcity mentality is the greatest limitation to our incredible potential. Believing you have something to lose or that you need to take away from others to experience all that life has to offer can only short-circuit your potential.

Having a true abundance mindset removes the limitations of our inherent beliefs. True abundance means living without the fear of losing. Because in the end, if you are living your purpose you cannot lose. You cannot lose because you are tapping into your best self.

APPLICATION

Through experience, we develop resilience. This resilience - more than happiness - is what will define us. Life isn't binary. It's not black and white. At every turn, we are changing the game. We're creating a new filter with which our decisions will be based.

We can take a proactive approach and help create a filter of abundance by believing. Through mantras and prayer, we can program our mind to think limitless. We can remind ourselves every morning and every night that we all have a divine purpose.

We all have a unique potential that is equally valuable.

The countless stories of amazing people that persevered can serve as other sources of inspiration when all seems dark. The stories of blind people running triathlons. The stories of single mothers raising three kids while working to provide them with a better life. The stories of orphans who become CEOs and change the world.

Don't allow this insight to only sink in when you face similar circumstances as my dear friend Brad. Treat it as a gift that you can enjoy now. I have.

PRAYER

Grant me the resilience and grit to handle life's bumps along the way.

DAILY DECLARATION

The imperfections in life are what make life perfect, for it's the imperfections that provide teaching moments. #FaithIntoAbundance

MEET GARY LEBLANC

Gary LeBlanc - recognized as an international thought leader - coaches individuals towards finding their purpose. Although Gary found success in the corporate world, his former career as a Vice President for a Tier 1 company left him searching for his own purpose.

When a close friend was diagnosed with cancer eight years ago, Gary realized that helping people live their best life was more than just an interest; it was his passion. Spending the better part of 20 years researching the latest diet, health, and fitness trends, Gary now empowers people to live their purpose.

Through his company Ikkuma Inc., Gary is focused on living his purpose by helping people Be SuperHuman. A McGill University Engineering and MBA graduate, Gary is also a certified coach practitioner, personal trainer, and most recently, a published author, with his book titled 'Ikkuma: Evolution of Vitality'.

Between dreaming about SuperHumans, making awesome smoothies and researching, Gary FaceTime's his beyond-cool niece and nephew. Gary is an in-demand speaker and author, who has now found his true purpose… helping you be your SuperHuman.

CONTACT GARY

Ikkuma

WEBSITE
Ikkuma.com

FACEBOOK
Facebook.com/Gary.LeBlanc.5209

INSTAGRAM
@ikkumaGary

TWITTER
@IkkumaGary

LINKEDIN
LinkedIn.com/in/IkkumaGary

WHY DID GOD TAKE MY DAD AND MY BUSINESS AWAY

DAN VALLEE

"The LORD is close to the brokenhearted and saves those who are crushed in spirit."

Psalm 34:18

I grew up as an only child. I was blessed to have an amazing Mom and Dad that loved me and provided me with everything that I ever needed.

My family has been in the real estate business ever since I was a very young boy, so naturally, when I graduated high school I became a real estate agent. Then, shortly after that, I became a real estate broker.

Over the years, my family and I grew the company into a multi-office real estate firm, along with a mortgage brokerage business. The income was flying in. There was no shortage of money and life was great. Anything we needed, we could have. I felt like I was in control of my life and I was king of the hill.

In 2001, my father went for a check up and was diagnosed with stage four bladder cancer. The doctors said that he had a 40% chance of living six months at the max. He instructed my mother and me to prepare funeral arrangements.

For weeks, I barely slept. I began to search for solutions to fight this battle, to get rid of this cancer and get my Dad's health back. For the first time in my life, I did not feel in control. I felt helpless and I did not know what to do.

Time was flying by with no solutions, so I turned to God and I prayed. I asked Him for help, and He did. God led us to another doctor who gave us hope.

With the right plan of action and several surgeries, including chemo and natural therapy, my dad's health started improving and his cancer went into remission. I was ecstatic. My mom was happy. We thanked God each day for His mercy. My dad was doing so great that no one would have known he ever had cancer. Life was great again and business was booming. I was back in control of my own destiny.

In July 2006, my mom, dad, and I went to Canada for a short vacation and to visit some of our relatives. While we were there, my dad's health started to decline at an extremely quick pace. We came back to Florida ready to fight the battle once again but this time we were not victorious. On September 4, 2006, my Dad went home to be with the Lord.

I could not understand why this had happened. I did not know why after everything my family and I had been through God still took my dad. I was very mad at Him.

In 2008, we experienced the worst economic period of our lifetime. At the time it felt like we had to deal with one tragedy after another.

At that point, I fell on my knees and I prayed. I asked God to take control of this situation. I had come to the realization that I was never in control and only God alone could solve this.

THE LESSON OF FAITH

I quickly learned that I needed to put God first, before anything else. As soon as I surrendered my life to him, I felt peace. All the stress that I was dealing with for many years was gone. I felt a ton of weight off my shoulders.

I knew at that point that God was in full control and that He loves me and that He had me in the palm of His hand. Over time, He molded me into the person that I am today.

I know that whatever situation comes my way, God can control. It doesn't matter how big of a trial I may be facing, God is bigger than any of them.

INTO ABUNDANCE

Putting God first in all areas of our life is key. God has restored our real estate and mortgage business. My mom and I are blessed to now have one of the fastest growing real estate firms in South Florida today. God is great. New agents are coming onboard every month. We have more clients than we can handle.

God brings forward new opportunities that we have never imagined before. He gives me all these creative ways to market and I know it comes from him. We are twice as busy than we were ever before the market crashed.

APPLICATION

When dealing with hard decisions, always pray first and listen for His guidance. He will always answer.

Sometimes God's answer may be for you just to be still. Trust Him and let Him guide you.

If you feel like it's not going the way that you planned or if the business is not going the way that you think it is going, do not get discouraged because He has bigger and better plans for your life.

PRAYER

Lord, I thank You that You are the God of the impossible. You can do anything. I want to trust in Your ability and not my own. Teach me to see difficulties in my life from Your perspective. Help me to focus on You and Your power.

DAILY DECLARATION

Sometimes God's answer may be for you just to be still.
#FaithIntoAbundance

MEET DAN VALLEE

Dan Vallee is an internationally known real estate authority, the author of several real estate books, the host of the online TV show Real Estate Boss and the CEO of Royal Florida Realty. Dan is a Certified Home Selling Advisor, which is a designation held by less than 1,000 real estate agents across the country.

Dan specializes in luxury properties and has a particular talent for moving property other realtors have failed to sell.

Dan has featured in Florida Realtor Magazine, on ABC, NBC, CBS News and Fox. Dan is also the co-creator of the "Real Estate office of the future" concept. With over 23 years experience as a Real Estate Broker and Loan Originator, Dan oversees 85 agents in his role as Chief Executive Officer in the high-tech firm Royal Florida Realty.

CONTACT DAN

Royal Florida Realty

WEBSITE

RoyalFloridaRealty.com

FACEBOOK

Facebook.com/DanVallee

INSTAGRAM

@royal_florida_realty

TWITTER

@DanVallee1

LINKEDIN

LinkedIn.com/in/Dan-Vallee-b456759

DAY 20

THE INEXPLICABLE VOID

BRANT PHILLIPS

> *"May the God of hope fill you with all joy and peace in believing, so that by the power of the Holy Spirit you may abound in hope."*
>
> *Rom. 15:13*

I was raised in a Christian household and spent a significant part of my young life in the church learning the ins and outs of Christianity; however, by the time I reached my twenties I had strayed very far away from God. After college, I had a blossoming career and was climbing the corporate ladder. I also got married around this time and soon after we had our first child.

So many great things were happening in my life. I had a corporate job, trophy wife, and my first child. From the outside, it may have looked as though I was living a seemingly perfect life, but it surely didn't feel like that on the inside. I felt that something was missing from my life, and it kept me from being able to completely enjoy all the wonderful things that were happening to and around me.

This inexplicable void that was taking hold of me had become so daunting that it led me to seek God once again in hopes of figuring out what exactly was wrong with me. It turned out that as my new relationship with God grew stronger, the void I was feeling grew smaller.

Also during that time, I was ready to leave my well-paying corporate job to get into the real estate business, which at the time was crashing and burning. I remember close family members and friends saying things like, "What the hell are you doing man?" or "What's wrong with you?" I wasn't able to explain it to them or even to myself.

Leaving my secure career to walk into the unventured territory that was a collapsing real estate market and being unsure if I would be able to pay my bills or support my family was a giant leap of faith, but I had to follow my heart, and I did.

THE LESSON OF FAITH

God speaks to us in many ways, and one of those ways is by calling us to action. Sometimes that calling may come with hardships and obstacles, but we should consider them as part of the blessing that God is bestowing upon us. There is a scripture in the Bible that tells us God plants seeds inside of us, but it is up to us to do the work necessary to turn that seed into fruit, or rewards.

INTO ABUNDANCE

I mentioned before that when I first felt that I was called to be an entrepreneur, I could not explain why. As the months and years passed, it became clearer that part of my purpose was to help others. Once I began to build my online presence via social media, people began to reach out to me seeking help and guidance with the issues I once struggled with myself.

This was my opportunity to respond to the calling that was teaching, coaching, and motivating others to be successful in their personal lives as well as with their businesses. Over the years I have developed several projects with that goal in mind.

The project I am most excited about and that I've had the most fun with is called "Breakthrough at the Beach." I like to describe it as a men's business boot camp. We train men in a retreat-like environment. We teach them how to live by a code that we call the "F4," which is a system that focuses on the daily investment of their faith, family, fitness, and finances.

APPLICATION

Whether it is building your faith or stepping into a new or unfamiliar business venture, it all starts with using that figurative seed inside of you and taking the necessary steps to turn that seed into fruit. If you feel that what you are doing is a God-inspired mission and something you are certain is for you, then go after it. I could not have accomplished all that I have done over the years without God being there by my side and helping me along the way.

PRAYER

Dear God, thank you for the gift of life and the opportunities before me. Help me to be a good steward with all that you've given me, and thank you for the people and resources you have provided me. Help me to stay obedient to your will and continue to be a force for good and a voice for your word.

DAILY DECLARATION

Life can be complicated. The Truth is not. Listen to the voice of Truth, and follow where it leads. #FaithIntoAbundance

MEET BRANT PHILLIPS

Brant is a full-time real estate investor, business owner, entrepreneur, author, and speaker. He has been featured on Fox News, hosts local seminars and is even being considered to star in one of those "Flipping Houses" TV shows.

Brant is a proverbial 'rags to riches' story. While living in an apartment and having no money, Brant was able to purchase his first investment property on a credit card! He went on to by ten properties that same year with no money down. In the last few years, he has rehabbed hundreds of homes and now owns a portfolio of rental properties worth millions. He routinely flips houses for fast cash.

Brant is a former police officer who prides himself on integrity and serving others. He is a husband and father of four and enjoys helping and teaching people to experience the freedom and success he has achieved through successfully investing in real estate.

CONTACT BRANT

Invest Home Pro

WEBSITE
InvestHomePro.com
BrantPhillips.com

FACEBOOK
Facebook.com/BrantAPhillips

INSTAGRAM
@brantaphillips

TWITTER
@tweetbrant

LINKEDIN
LinkedIn.com/in/BrantPhillips

THE DAY I LOST MY
SENSE OF SMELL

PATSY RAE DAWSON

"For the Lord will not cast off forever, but, though he cause grief, he will have compassion according to the abundance of his steadfast love; for he does not willingly afflict or grieve the children of men."

Lamentations 3:31-33

Big white teeth. Big White Teeth! BIG WHITE TEETH! Five inches from my 7-year-old face! My mother's hot, bad-smelling breath smothered me as she screamed, "I hate you! I wish you were never born!"

An old picture reveals a cute, lively, bossy little girl with her hands on her hips. I loved to laugh and play chase with my two brothers.

Then one fateful day my life changed forever....

Mother and I were at my grandparents' house when someone found my teenage aunt's note.... My uncle and grandfather pounded on the bathroom door and then busted it open. I followed as each took an arm and dragged my aunt through the house out into the yard. I watched them shake her and holler, "Breathe! Breathe!"

Quietly...I slipped back to the bathroom. I stepped inside. Uuhhhhh....
I gasped as the lingering rotten-egg odor of gas from the bathroom
heater burned my nose.... And my memories stop.

Within weeks, my grandparents moved with my aunt to a distant state.
They left their youngest son in the care of his older brother to finish
high school. At age 7, I lost my only source of hugs.

I changed almost overnight as my personality masked. I seldom
laughed. I became painfully shy. My terrified subconscious refused to
smell my mother's hate-filled breath blasting my face...so I could
continue to love my mother who did not love me.

In the process, I lost the ability to smell anything at all.

When I married and got away from my mother's screaming, my
genetic humor and ease around people started to come back. But
within months, the old mask began to return. I had gone from one
unloving home to another of a different kind. Without awareness, I
retreated into survival mode so I could love my husband who refused
to show love for me.

Forty-six years later, I divorced. Before the divorce finalized, my
spontaneous laughter returned. I delighted to discover I'm naturally
outgoing. Although I could remember some smells before age 7, my
sense of smell did not return.

That changed one fateful evening in a writers' critique meeting about
a year later. We were evaluating another writer's romance. A male
writer commented that her scene of the man and woman meeting was
boring. He explained, "A man is drawn in by appearance. You need to
make it more interesting."

"But this is a Christian romance. The editors won't stand for much of
that."

"I understand. But you need to show us why he's attracted to her. Men love smells. What perfume is she wearing?"

His innocent comment upset me. I've been teaching and writing about the Song of Solomon for over forty years. It's the Bible's love story to teach us how to love and enjoy passionate sex for a lifetime.... And it's full of smells. The only thing I know about smells is what someone tells me or I read.

My soul cried—I want to smell love!

And so the journey began to face the truth of why I could not smell. I contacted a Christian counselor friend to help me remember...and deal with my childhood.

Six months later, at age 66, I was plunging a stopped-up toilet. I flashed back to the sight of blood and something floating in the toilet. I shook my head. The flashback disappeared. I plunged again. I dropped the plunger. I gasped as my embedded memory of the unspeakable horror made me run outside into the sun.

My mother's screams followed me, "I wish you were never born!"

Within days, I recognized my first smell—the sharp odor released from slicing an onion. Working with my counselor to examine my childhood through adult eyes, I continued to experience new smells with each victory.

Months later for the first time in my life, I smelled love in a gift of potted red poises. They fascinated me with the distinctive smells of the three stages of bloom—the bud's strong alluring fragrance, the flower's mellow aroma, and the wilting petals' fading scent.

THE LESSON OF FAITH

Years earlier, I had become a certified Advanced Personality Trainer in Wired That Way. I discovered that the two personality squares I absolutely knew were not mine were indeed my 60% genetic self. You see, the remaining 40% nurturing can be so terrible, as in my case, that it overpowers our genetic personality.

Instead of being a masked codependent peacemaking Phlegmatic, I'm a natural laughing, outgoing Sanguine who enjoys stirring up life. Rather than being a slightly depressed Melancholy who strives to be perfect to avoid being screamed at, I'm an organized can-do Choleric who thinks 75% perfect is good enough.

Recently, while working with a business coach we explored my brand and business personality. She helped me see that through masking, I had mastered the Phlegmatic's wise Sage. I also excelled at the Melancholy's Maverick who instigates change to make the world a better place.

After I had lost my grandparents' hugs, I dared to assert that my brothers and I deserved a better mother. My mother responded with slaps, ridicule, or cruel punishment. But until I graduated from high school, I continued to challenge her abusive authority as I contemplated how to win her affection.

My coach explained, "Your Maverick gives you the self-confidence to speak comfortably about a forbidden topic. That's why your fans call you, 'The most outspoken Christian woman on sex.' You became a Maverick to fight for survival. Now God uses your Maverick side to fight for others who desperately need your message about how to survive and overcome the #1 Googled marriage problem—sexless marriages."

Resentment gave way to deeper forgiveness of my mother.

A few days later, God rewarded my spiritual growth with a new sensation. I was making chicken stir-fry with onions, summer and zucchini squash, celery, and spinach. I love to cook and experiment. But being unable to smell dulls one's taste buds. I can't taste food and tell what spices it needs. Consequently, I usually cook by a recipe.

This time, I was just throwing it together. I generously added minced garlic, fresh cilantro, and chipotle seasoning along with sea salt and pepper. It tasted flat. For the first time in my life, I KNEW what it needed—Italian seasoning and cumin!

INTO ABUNDANCE

Our senses of smell and taste along with our personalities and sexual responses are emotionally driven. For forty years, I taught women and men the secret of our brain for more intimacy in marriage. Now I've become living proof of the power of one's thoughts and emotions over all these sensations.

I became gutsier in teaching mothers and fathers how to love each other and their children in my new book. I shared how hormones of love can bond husbands and wives together. This creates a hugging, kissing, loving family environment for them and their children.

Experiencing the smell of love as a gift from God spurred me on to launch a free new program. The eye-opening questionnaire covers first generational narcissism in families of origin, second generational naivety and clustered love sins in marriages, third generational enabling and narcissism in children, and fourth generational potential harm to grandchildren.

I'm fighting for every child to be raised by parents who love each other…and their children.

APPLICATION

Are you masked? Are you painfully shy? Are you neglecting your gifts from God of personality and character because you're living in survival mode?

While our childhood shapes us, it's only the beginning of who we're meant to be. Spend time in prayer asking God to open your eyes to your personal truths. Take the best of what the worst spawned and add it to your genetic self. Only then can you dare to rise to your full potential in loving your family and others.

PRAYER

"Dear Lord, thank you for preserving my authentic personality in my DNA. Thank you for allowing the traumas of life to enrich my character and use it to fulfill your ultimate plan. Please continue to open my eyes to your wisdom and love so that I can speak out boldly to your glory."

DAILY DECLARATION

God preserves our authentic self in our DNA. When we resolve our childhood, He rewards us with enriched character.
#FaithIntoAbundance

MEET PATSY RAE DAWSON

Patsy Rae Dawson, an International marriage consultant, has mentored both husbands and wives for over 40 years. Her expertise ranges from the joys of soulmating to the beautiful sexual teachings of the Song of Solomon to the complex issues of difficult marriages. Her unique ability to unlock the scriptures and challenge traditional views makes Patsy a popular speaker and writer.

Her readers describe her as gutsy, bold, and the most outspoken Christian woman on sex, referring to her frankness and not holding anything back.

Patsy is known as the lady who asks too many questions. Her dad liked to say, "As a child, when everyone else was laughing at my story, Patsy would ask, Is that the truth?"

Continuing to ask that question throughout her life, plus searching for answers for her students, has led Patsy on some amazing journeys and discoveries. One preacher said, "I'm reading your Song of Solomon material again and am continually amazed at your insights."

Patsy's 26 writing awards include First Place at the prestigious Texas Christian Writers Conference in Houston for Challenges in Marriage: What to Do When Sin Inhibits Love and First Place with The Song of Solomon: God's Sex Education.

PatsyRaeDawson.com deals with the good, the bad, and the ugly facing modern marriages. Her Embarrass the Alligator newsletter at EmbarrasstheAlligator.com, with columns Ask PatsyRae and Tips for Alligator Wrestling, tells it like it is and showcases her keen insight.

CONTACT PATSY

WEBSITE
PatsyRaeDawson.com

FACEBOOK
Facebook.com/PatsyRaeDawson.LLC

LINKEDIN
LinkedIn.com/in/PatsyRae

TWITTER
@PatsyRae

DAY 22

UNSTOPPABLE CHRISTIAN

DR. RON ECCLES

> *"For I know the plans I have for you, declares the Lord, plans to prosper you and not harm you, plans to give you hope and a future."*
>
> *Jeremiah 29:11*

It was no ordinary Mastermind. On this particular sunny Florida day and I was standing in front of around 30 smart business owners and about to have them grill me.

Masterminds are groups of like-minded people, typically business owners, gathering together several times a year to share ideas and resources to help grow each other's businesses.

Each member had 40 minutes to share what their business was about, how it worked and where they needed help.

I was friends with most of the members and had a great deal of respect for them. There was only one other business owner in the room that was a devout follower of Christ.

As I began my presentation, I asked the group to look for areas where I might narrow my focus to a more specific niche or target group of people to serve in my business.

I had been a professional speaker and business coach for several years and was having difficulty defining my ideal audience. Up until that point, I was serving all demographics – both business owners and non-business owners.

I was very much aware that attempting to "speak" to everyone usually means you wind up speaking to no one.

Less than five minutes into my talk, one of the Mastermind members raised his hand and said, "Dr. Ron…you need to be in the Christian space"! Instantly there was a resounding "Yes!" from the group. Everyone agreed.

Like so many men and women before me who have heard the call of God in their lives and ignore it, I quickly dismissed the idea using the rational that I wanted my message to be shared to all people, not just Christians.

It wasn't until about two years later that I began to hear that call once again and I decided to make a shift and move some of my speaking and coaching to the Christian businessmen and women. This time, I was ready to obey!

I decided to create a new brand to launch into the Christian business community and came up with "Unstoppable Christian."

Shortly after making this decision, I was having lunch with the young man (Ben) from the Mastermind that raised his hand and suggested I bring my business more into the Christian arena.

During lunch, I shared with Ben my decision to launch "Unstoppable Christian." My plan was to move more of my speaking and coaching into that brand. Ben saw it differently!

About an hour after our lunch together, I received a text message from Ben saying "Unstoppable Christian" is the BIGGEST idea you've ever had. I quickly call him to hear what was on his mind.

Ben said that "Unstoppable Christian" wasn't a small business relegated to some coaching and speaking. He saw it as a worldwide movement. Something people could rally around. He envisioned (keep in mind, Ben is not a believer) people from all over the planet sharing the same faith gathering for "Unstoppable Christian" concerts, men's retreats, women's retreats, marriage conferences, teen-oriented events, prayer groups, etc.

I was instantly overwhelmed at the thought of leading such a large movement. I shuttered at the thought of the massive undertaking. My mind was fixed on how big the challenge was and the time, resources and talent that would be required.

Here is where I would love to claim that my enthusiasm and excitement propelled me headfirst into the task ahead...but that's not what happened!

My mistake (once again) was that God was speaking and I wasn't listening. All I could see was how big the mountain was to climb!

Several weeks later during my morning devotion, God began to softly whisper in my ear. I heard His loving voice say, "Aren't you the one who keeps praying to Me 'Here I am Lord, use me as you will'?" "Are you available for Me or not?" is all I could hear.

That morning, my response was different. God began to open my eyes to see things differently. My vision shifted from one of how big the challenge was to "How Big My God Is!"

I finally realized that it wasn't me that would be leading, but my Savior, the Creator of the universe, Jesus.

All I had to do was step out in faith and watch God move.

My wife Johanna and I launched our Facebook Fan Page "Unstoppable Christian" along with our website in January of 2016.

We also host *Unstoppable Christian Radio* every Saturday from 11am-12pm EST (available on the app FaithTalk 570&910 WTBN).

I'm in the process of writing the book "The Seven Habits of Unstoppable Christians."

Our first event is planned for early 2017 in the Tampa Bay area of Florida. It will be targeted to Christian Business Owners and the theme will be "Immeasurably More" from Ephesians 3:20-21.

He leads...we follow

THE LESSON OF FAITH

The Bible is full of stories of how God uses ordinary men and women to accomplish His sovereign plans. Too often we hear the call of God on our lives and we dismiss it simply because we are focused on the wrong thing...ourselves! I'm not smart enough, not gifted in that area, to poor, not the right color, ethnicity or pedigree.

How we see ourselves and our situation in life often deters us from stepping into the will of God!

When we take on a new perspective and see the story of our lives (our past) as the preparation or training ground for God to mold us into who He wants us to be so He can use us for His purposes, we will begin to walk in His power!

Like the apostle Peter, God beacons us out of the boat and to follow Him. When we keep our eyes on Jesus and not the circumstances of life, we will walk on water. By listening to the call of God on your life, you will need to rely on God's daily provision of Grace as you step forward, one step at a time.

INTO ABUNDANCE

In Jeremiah 29:11 we learn of God's intention toward us. The Scripture is filled with around 7,000 promises. They are all "CONDITIONAL" upon us doing our part.

God uses men and women, young and old, weak or strong, poor or rich to fulfill His will. When He calls, simply obey, step out in faith and trust that God will provide all we need. He's calling you and me!

Johanna and I are watching God provide. He has brought dozens of other believers into our lives who have a desire to help us grow the "Unstoppable Christian" movement. We believe God will provide us with all the talent and resources needed to serve the community of believers throughout the world.

We remain fully submitted to His plan and will faithfully follow knowing that He will bring about the increase!

APPLICATION

You and I were made for a purpose. Our greatest reason for existing is to Love and Worship God and to be Loved by Him. God has equipped each of us with a unique combination of talents and gifts that no one that has ever existed in history, no one living today and no one ever to be born will have.

God will call us all to do something for Him. When you hear his voice, simply obey! Step out into the unknown with faith and claim the grace needed to walk in His power.

Sometimes God whispers, sometimes He shouts and sometimes He speaks to us through others, even unbelievers.

PRAYER

Father, I am yours, made in your image and my life has meaning. I believe that you have plans to prosper me according to your will and the Glory of Your Kingdom. Open my ears and eyes that I might hear and see what you are doing and grant me the faith to boldly step out and obey your call.

DAILY DECLARATION

When God calls; listen and obey. His plans are to use you just the way you are. #FaithIntoAbundance

MEET DR. RON ECCLES

Ron became part of Make Your Mark as lead trainer for the United States in 2015. Laying down the groundwork for a solid start, he and his wife Johanna are a "Heart Centered" team bringing MYM the "Business with SOUL" first to Tampa Bay, Florida. Ron's WHY is to contribute to a greater cause, to inspire others to maximum achievement. I do this by making sense out of the complicated and helping you get to the real problem so you can finally resolve what has been keeping you back. Known as "The Success Doctor" Ron is a professional speaker/Author/ Business Coach traveling throughout the US and abroad inspiring others.

He believes that we are all created to be financially free, to have a leaner more fit & healthier body, to enjoy deep loving relationships and a powerful spiritual walk. Dr. Ron has 33 years of business experience as a entrepreneur and has practiced as a doctor of chiropractic (He is board certified in Orthopedics and Neurology). He was a post grad faculty teacher for 4 different chiropractic schools.

He has owned and operated several businesses over the past three plus decades including restaurants, DVD vending machines and real estate investing. He now spends his time devoted to speaking, coaching business owners, consulting and writing. He and his wife, Johanna, mother and sister, reside in Lakewood Ranch Florida. He is the proud father of 5 children, which are all grown and out on their own. He and his wife love working out every day, going to the movies and eating Thai food!

Their church and faith play a large part in their lives. Dr. Ron is passionate about seeing others reach the full potential they were created for.

He is a dedicated "Success Coach," Speaker and Author with more then three decades of experience and training.

CONTACT RON

Unstoppable Christian

LINKEDIN
LinkedIn.com/in/DrRonEccles

INSTAGRAM
@UnstoppableChristianWorldWide

TWO DOLLARS IN MY HUBCAP

MATT LACLEAR

> *"Cast your cares on the Lord and he will sustain you; he will never let the righteous be shaken."*
>
> *Psalm 55:22*

Our son Timothy was born with severe jaundice. We were young parents and didn't have much money. We were living with my mother-in-law, who happened to live across the street from my parents.

We live in Michigan and the weather at that time of year was subzero. Timothy had a doctor's appointment, but our old van was low on gas, and we had no money to fill it up.

My wife and I had our own business then, but it was struggling badly. Usually when we needed help, we would borrow money from either my mother-in-law or my parents, but unfortunately for us, neither of them were around at that time. My wife and I end up getting into an argument over whether or not we should still go despite the van being so low on gas. "Well I guess we are going anyway," she said. I replied, "Well we're going to run out of gas." We ended up deciding to take the risk and went anyway.

To our surprise, we made it all the way to the doctor's office without running out of gas. As soon as we pulled into the parking lot, however, the van started shaking and shuddering like cars do right before they run out of gas. We took Timothy inside so he could be seen by the doctor. During the visit, I couldn't help but wonder how we would get home.

Upon leaving my wife said to me "God will provide a way home." As we were getting into the van, something caught my wife's eye. In the hubcap of the front tire was two one dollar bills that must have blown across were parking lot and somehow got stuck in the van's hubcap. That two dollars paid for enough gas to get us back home, and it was the best two dollars I had ever spent.

THE LESSON OF FAITH

God is a god of solutions. A lot of people may feel despair both in their lives and with their businesses because they don't notice the solutions that our loving God is trying to bless them with.

We brothers and sisters in Christ all have our respective problems. Whether the issue is a past-due phone bill, a wayward child, a sick child, a layoff, or a shut off or broken down vehicle, there is always a solution. That solution is Jesus Christ.

Although we may not be able to see or feel him around us, He is always there.

INTO ABUNDANCE

In times of worry and despair, we just close our eyes and know that the solution to the problem exists. God provides how He provides. What we do expect is that there will be a favorable outcome.

We just equate it to the two dollars that we needed when we needed it. We just go to Him, and He's always there. Always.

So many times we have come so close to hitting the ground. You think that you're falling, and you're going to hit the ground and that's going to be the end of it. You know what? We never hit.

APPLICATION

Understand that your faith is power. Psalm 55:22 tells us that if we cast our cares on the Lord, He will sustain us both in our personal lives and with our businesses. It is Him that runs our businesses. It is Him that brings clients through our doors. It is Him that makes those clients return. It is Him that enables us to be able to pay our bills and take care of ourselves and our families.

MEET MATT LACLEAR

Almost every SEO agent you speak to these days will do their level best to convince you of their ability to be able to fool Google and the other search engines into pushing your site to the top of the search result pages.

You won't hear anything of the sort from me anymore though.

Sure there was a time not too long ago when I felt the best way to generate revenue for a client was to use black hat methods to fool the search engine algorithms into giving our clients better rankings.

The problem with that philosophy was and still remains to be two fold. First, focusing only on generating increases in ranks totally ignores the conversion process that has to take place in order for a website to generate income. Second, by focusing only on improving rankings via black hat methods client' sites are far more open to penalties, algorithmic drops and all other kinds of nasty crawly things that will keep you up at night.

Now we focus more on boosting our clients' revenue by dramatically improving their conversion mechanisms and processes.

Once the conversions are in place we start grafting in sources of targeted traffic from the search engines, PPC, social media sites, YouTube and anywhere else prospects are hanging out online these days.

Engineering real profit from a website or web properties takes a lot of hard work and painstaking attention to detail.

CONTACT MATT

Your Ad Squad

WEBSITE
YourAdSquad.com

FACEBOOK
Facebook.com/Matt.LaClear.3

TWITTER
@MattLaClear

DAY 24

IF YOU LEAVE

ASHLEY HILL

> *"Therefore do not worry about tomorrow, for tomorrow will worry about itself. Each day has enough trouble of its own."*
>
> *Matthew 6:34*

"I'm just done. God, I'm done." This was my breaking point in the ongoing tragedy that had become my marriage and my life. I had been married to a pastor with whom I was living overseas. It sounds like the beginning of a beautiful story, and it was; however, the story did not turn out as beautifully as it had begun. What started as a fulfilling and promising marriage gradually turned into an empty, abusive one.

I remember the exact point that I decided I could not continue to remain in the dark place to which my husband and marriage had driven me. I had returned home from work, and almost immediately the yelling began. The atmosphere was hostile and chaotic, and the reason why was beyond me.

At that exact moment, I had understood that my life had spun entirely out of control. I was tired of doing what I call 'playing church,' something I had been doing almost all my life being the daughter of ministers. I knew how to robotically quote scriptures with everybody and pretend to be happy, but I had reached such a low point that it all had to stop.

I didn't have any more answers. I had run out of methods of dealing with this turbulence in my life. I needed God to step in my life and do it quickly. I dropped to my knees and began to pray.

"God, what is this?" I asked. "I'm not used to being in this kind of situation. It's uncomfortable. It's painful." Everything that I was feeling came out in my prayer.

Suddenly, in the same toxic, catastrophic atmosphere where my husband and I were fighting, I felt the presence of God. Once I felt Him, His spirit began to fill the room completely. A moment before, I had wanted to be angry and lash out in rage against my husband, but almost instantaneously I felt calm and peaceful. God spoke to me.

"You need to leave," He instructed. "I promise I will take care of you," He assured me. While I knew this was the best solution, a part of me wanted to stay and fight for my marriage. I wanted control. I wanted to fix my marriage.

I started to bargain with God. I said to him, "Oh, God, if I pray more I know You will fix this."

He unwaveringly repeated His instruction, "If You leave I will take care of you. I will take care of it all." I wasn't able to trust and believe God entirely, but eventually I decided to go out on a limb and follow His lead. A few months later, I left my husband.

When I reflect back today, I see that this painful, destructive, and violent part of my life was all a part of God's overall plan for my life as well as my business.

THE LESSON OF FAITH

I learned something I should have known long before; that God is and has always been in control. I have control over my life, but only to a certain extent. God has the final say, which is why once I had run out of options of my own I had none other to turn to but God. That is the best option I could have.

INTO ABUNDANCE

It is interesting how I have come to be able to use things I learned in such an unhealthy marriage to help me maintain a healthy business. When I was married, I had a habit of trying to use different tips, tricks, and new methods to make things work. I made that same habit useful with my business.

I would think, "Okay, I'm struggling. I'm a new business and I need clients." I would then use all the tips I came across before. I would call and consult so-called experts, who would tell me to try this or try that. A lot of the times none of their suggestions ended up helping me much.

When I got to a point where I was tired of being stressed out and losing sleep over not knowing what to do, I realized my best decision was to make God my CEO. I was the CEO on paper, but I had to make God the CEO in spirit, and pray to Him for direction and control, something I did not have in either my business or my marriage.

I began to seek God's instruction much more. I started to spend more time in His word. I invested in him fully, which included me spending more time in church and being more involved in church activities.

I can confidently say that because of taking those steps toward making God the center of my business, I have made more money in the past six months than I ever have in my full six years of being in business.

To this very day, God is at the center of my business. I check in with Him regarding work as much as I do regarding my personal life. I find myself asking Him, "God, do you want me to take this contract?" or "Should I go to this conference and meet with so and so?" Sometimes His answer is ambiguous, and other times it is a clear response. I thank God that I am able to avoid certain failures and/or disappointments as a result of his guidance.

APPLICATION

All my fellow Christian entrepreneurs should understand that they as well have to make God their CEO. Your success and the success of your business are in God's hand. You have to allow Him to take that role and then align with Him in what He wants you to do.

Although I would say that one of the most important aspects of business is profit, of course, as Christian entrepreneurs we should hold being God's witnesses as just as important. God wants to use us and our businesses to reach the lost. If you allow Him to use you, you will be able to both make a profit and impact lives.

PRAYER

God, help us to align with your perfect will for our lives so that we can fulfill our purpose in the Earth. In Jesus Name, Amen

DAILY DECLARATION

I am valuable. I am limitless. I will not fear. I am loved. I am a powerful being. No weapon formed against me shall prosper. God is working everything out for my good. #FaithIntoAbundance

MEET ASHLEY HILL

Ashley Hill is a Scholarship Search Strategist and CEO of ALH Group LLC. She is passionate about teaching overwhelmed students (K-12, homeschool, adult, international, undergraduate, and graduate students) how to use their talents and achievements to increase their chances of winning scholarships. She is the author of The Ultimate Guide for Finding and Winning More Money for College.

CONTACT ASHLEY

FACEBOOK
Facebook.com/Prep4College

LINKEDIN
LinkedIn.com/in/AshleyLHill

TWITTER
@prepforcollege

INSTAGRAM
@ashleylhill24

DAY 25

THE 99 YARD MARK

JOHN ROWLEY

> *"My comfort in my suffering is this: Your promise preserves my life."*
>
> *Psalm 119:50*

I lost everything. I had no car, my house was under foreclosure, and I had no source of income.

I lost a business and I was very, very deep in debt. My future looked bleak. Everything was awful. But, I was getting up every morning still believing God would make something work for me

I am an author, and at the time I was working on a few books while simultaneously trying to find a job. I tried my hardest but for some reason I just could not find work to save my life. Although I was extremely discouraged, I never lost faith that God would create an opportunity for me.

For five years, I would get together with my pastor two or three times a week. He'd say, "You're at the 99 yard mark."

I said, "No, you told me that three years ago."

I was on the 99 yard mark for five years, and we lost absolutely everything...even my marriage.

Eventually God came through, and provided a business opportunity that is now a multi-million dollar endeavor.

THE LESSON OF FAITH

It's so much easier to give up when you don't have scripture, when you don't have God to lean on, or when you don't have faith in God. He didn't guide me the way I wanted, nor did He give me the answer I wanted.

I would have liked for Him to just snap his fingers and make everything better instantly. But it didn't work like that. I came to realize that while I didn't feel Him working in my life at the time, He was always right there by my side.

INTO ABUNDANCE

My business is to use health, fitness, and motivation to create a platform from which I can bring Christ into the world and into the lives of the people. I use several different mediums to help these individuals receive the gospel, including motivational videos and Christian books. My purpose is using my career as a not only a way to make a living but to be a messenger for God and the word of God.

APPLICATION

I think every Christian entrepreneur at least understands that everything that we have is from God. Our business is from God, the profit that comes in from our business is from God, and the way we handle those profits should be in a way that is pleasing to God.

PRAYER

Gracious God, grant us open minds and open hearts to receive your grace and wisdom. Through the power of our Holy Spirit dwelling in us, may we have the courage to face life's challenges and the resilience to remain faithful. Give us eyes to see your vision for how we might love one another and have reverence for all your creation. All this we pray in the name of the one who calls us to follow him, Jesus the Christ. Amen.

DAILY DECLARATION

My business is from God, and I declare that the way I handle those profits will be in a way that is pleasing to God. #FaithIntoAbundance

MEET JOHN ROWLEY

When a devastating car accident cut his promising college athletic career short, John had a choice. He could give up his dream and accept the fate others thought he was doomed to, or search out a new course to better his life. So, he did what winners do. He faced the challenge and conquered his limitations.

Determined to be healthy again, he took on recovery with a vengeance, studying kinesiology, exercise, anatomy, fitness and nutrition. It was an attitude that would serve him well the rest of his life. It enabled John to work his way up from a janitor in Brooklyn to the high-powered world of New York City real estate. Stretching his entrepreneurial wings, he bought the Brooklyn gym featured in the movie Pumping Iron – starring famed body builders Arnold Schwarzenegger and Lou Ferrigno. John went on to combine his unique knowledge and his passion to help people with his run-away best seller, Old School New Body. John has also released The UX3 Perfect Meal Formula – a comprehensive meal strategy for those who are looking for optimal fitness results.

CONTACT JOHN

Rowley's Results Unlimited

WEBSITE
UX3Nutrition.com

FACEBOOK
Facebook.com/RowleyJM

YOU AREN'T QUALIFIED TO DO THIS

PHILLIP SINGLETON

"Lord, show me my end and the measure of my days, so I will know how frail I am."

Psalms 39: 4

It was May 22nd at 4:03 pm. I was online in my office at my former job checking my social media accounts. I scrolled through Facebook and browsed Instagram.

Suddenly, there was a spirit that came over me and told me to eliminate all distractions. I said to myself, "Okay, I'm going to go on a forty-two day fast and see what happens after that."

I started reading Rick Warren's "Purpose Driven Life" and although I didn't know it at the time, it ended up helping me find my walk and purpose in life.

I reached the fortieth day of my fast and still I had no luck. I had a job interview a couple of days before but was turned down. I spoke aloud, "God, I am not going anywhere until you move me."

After eighty-five days, I came to the realization that I should step out on my faith and start my own business. Eliminating my distractions allowed me to open up my mind and my ability.

THE LESSON OF FAITH

I learned that God blesses each of us with our individual gifts and talents that nobody else has. Because I was battling a little bit of depression during my job hunt I often thought, "Why aren't I good enough? What's going on? I'm frustrated in this situation. I'm living check to check. I'm mad at my job. I'm just mad in general because I'm not progressing."

What I learned from that is that God's timing is perfect and at the same time I had to stay steadfast and lean more on my faith than my time.

Understanding that God took me on this journey for a reason, and all my skill sets and all the talents I needed, it needed to be grown in a certain time frame and certain period, so that when I did step out on faith and start my own business I had all the tools I needed through. God's intervention is helping me teach through life's lessons.

INTO ABUNDANCE

It's been something I've implemented because I know I wouldn't be on this journey right now as a young entrepreneur without taking that step out on faith. Every day I sit down and meditate. Not only to map out my business goals but where I want to be spiritually.

I've always implemented the teachings from that fast and everything I've done in my business, like putting God first.

I had a lot of naysayers try to hold me back. They would say, "You know what Philip, you're a young black lobbyist. This isn't a field where black people really get ahead. You don't know how to get clients. You don't even know how to do the job."

But I stayed guided in my faith, understanding that I'm here for a reason and God wouldn't just leave me here just to fall into a pit.

After all the negative things that were said, I was able to get my first client and successfully work for them. God has opened up so many doors; I've even been recognized as one of the top young Millennials in political consulting.

My resume has been boosted, my client roster has increased, and I've gotten the chance to prove myself and my business over and over.

APPLICATION

Like the Bible says, having the faith of a mustard seed is important. There will be times when your clients don't pay on time, you lose a contract, you struggle to gain new contracts or whatever it is in the specific field.

You must remember to stay faithful. It's not about the spoils, the money, or the clientele, but it about the value your God-given skills bring to other people. Whether it's through your work or any other area of your life, staying in the word and putting God first is the key to taking your business and life wherever you want it to go.

PRAYER

We pray to you God with the faith of a mustard seed, that all we do, all we say, all we think, and all we hope will take root in this world and be the source for of new expressions of your love, of your justice, of your character, of your mission, and of your kingdom.

DAILY DECLARATION

Remain humble and hungry. #FaithIntoAbundance

MEET PHILLIP SINGLETON

Phillip A. Singleton, founder of Singleton Consulting, opened the full service governmental affairs and multicultural outreach firm in September 2014. He previously served as Legislative Director for a law firm, providing clients with legislative guidance, culturally targeted messaging and strategic campaign outreach.

Mr. Singleton has a true passion for leadership and political success. Working with Fortune 500 companies, the Florida Legislature, collegiate sports teams, and the banking industry, Phillip has displayed his multi-talented skills. Over the years, he has gained a plethora of knowledge for diverse marketing strategies, the legislative process, as well as the nation's political climate.

In 2010, at the age of 24, he became the youngest African-American lobbyist in Florida history. During his time working in Florida's political process, Phillip has played an instrumental role in passing legislation regarding the expansion of Major League Soccer (MLS) in

Florida; National Background checks on for-hire chauffeurs; Campaign and Election Reform; advancing the Break Pay Scholarship for Post-9/11 G.I. Bill student veterans; along with securing millions in state funding for various local government economic development projects.

CONTACT PHILLIP

Singleton Consulting

WEBSITE
PhillipSingleton.com

FACEBOOK
Facebook.com/Phillip1.Singleton

LINKEDIN
LinkedIn.com/in/PhillipSingleton

TWITTER
@HipHopLobbyist

INSTAGRAM
@HipHopLobbyist

DAY 27

THE WEALTH OF STEWARDSHIP

BEN MALICK

> *"For if I do this voluntarily, I have a reward; but if against my will, I have a stewardship entrusted to me."*
>
> *1 Corinthians 9:17*

When I was in college, someone mentioned Dave Ramsey to me. Since I was a college student on a tight budget, I was like, "Let's check it out." So, I read a Dave Ramsey book and became sort of a budget nerd after that. Then I went down this path to the world of finance and money. Money became an idol for me. I thought, "If I start making this much money, I'll be happier."

Throughout my career, I had been shooting for a particular goal. When I reached it, I still felt like I wanted something more.

At that point, I realized that I was focusing on the wrong thing. I was working hard to become a portfolio manager, and I had finally reached that after years of study and work. But I felt like I wanted something more. I realized it was because I was focusing on getting what "I" wanted versus what God wanted for me.

About seven years into my financial career, I discovered a group called Kingdom Advisors founded by Ron Blue and Larry Burkett. It's a group of financial professionals seeking to help with people's finances, but in a biblical way. I connected with them, and learned what the Scripture says about money, possessions, and the idea of stewardship and applying that and making your life about stewardship.

THE LESSON OF FAITH

It's not about money or status; it's about being able to help people and how was I seeing myself doing that to serve others. Not that I wasn't able to do that in my career at that point in time, but I didn't view my job as serving others. It was a self-serving job to me.

I then learned the stewardship mindset. I was managing money for people. I was managing it to help them just build wealth but without any of the stewardship aspects even considered.

That was a revelation for me – this is God's money. What are we doing with it? What are the goals and how are we going to glorify God with the money, with the resources, with what he's given us? That's what we're called to do in anything take what God has given us and use it for

His glory.

INTO ABUNDANCE

Once I realized that, I left my six-figure job to start a business. I'm still in the midst of that whole process and in the early years of the business. It's entrepreneurial, so there is a lot of uncertainty.

It was a huge pay cut, but we trust in God, and we know that I'm viewing my job now in this business as a ministry. I want to help other people realize this stewardship mindset as well.

APPLICATION

God has given each of us gifts, resources, whatever you want to call it, and we're supposed to use these to maximize the kingdom impact while we have time here on this Earth. I think that others can look at their capabilities, resources, whether it is money or skills, time, whatever, and determine how can we use these to help others, and in essence, by helping others, glorify God.

I think all entrepreneurs obviously are not in business just to make a bunch of money, but the ones that are successful are the ones that are passionate about the people that they're helping and want to serve others well.

PRAYER

Thank you for being my loving Father. You own it all, yet you give freely. Everything I have is Yours. Show me how can I better manage what You've entrusted to me. Help me to use what You've given me for your glory and not my own. Give me an eternal perspective to do the work to which You've called me. I want to be a good steward and when my time comes I want to hear the words, "Well done good and faithful servant." I love you. Amen.

DAILY DECLARATION

Biblical financial stewardship is about more than just money. #FaithIntoAbundance

MEET BEN MALICK, CFA

Ben Malick is the founder of Three Nine Financial, a firm focused on helping clients live out their faith through the management of their financial resources. He loves helping others see how the Bible can be applied in all areas of life. This is not just a job for him; it's a ministry and a calling.

After graduating from Northwest Missouri State University with a degree in Financial Management, he started his first job in the financial industry in August of 2008. Since then, he's worked with many individuals and institutions, helping to manage their portfolios and providing investment advice. While working, he continued his education, earning an MBA from University of Kansas, and the Chartered Financial Analyst® designation, the most respected and recognized investment management designation in the world.

Several years into Ben's financial career, his eyes were opened to the concept of Biblically Responsible Investing (BRI). It's because of the convictions God placed on his heart regarding BRI that Ben felt led to start Three Nine Financial. He's passionate about educating others on why it's important to align their investment portfolios with biblical values, and how they can do so.

Through Three Nine Financial, Ben is on a mission to help stewards manage the resources entrusted to their care for maximum Kingdom impact.

CONTACT BEN

Three Nine Financial

WEBSITE
ThreenineFinancial.com

FACEBOOK
Facebook.com/ThreeNineFinancial

LINKEDIN
LinkedIn.com/in/BenJMalick

TWITTER
@39financial

DAY 28

BUT I'M AN ACTRESS!

ZONDRA WILSON

> *"Have I not commanded you? Be strong and courageous. Do not be afraid; do not be discouraged, for the LORD your God will be with you wherever you go."*
>
> *Joshua 1:9*

I felt a calling from God to move to Los Angeles to get into the acting industry. It was very difficult for me to be obedient and go.

Eventually, in 2004 I made the transition to moving to LA. I prayed and asked God, "Okay. Lord, why am I coming here?"

He would not give me the specifics. He just told me to go, which is how our God usually works.

Through my prayers, He told me that it wouldn't be easy. He said I would come up against opposition. But I had no clue what the oppositions would be.

In my mind, I would always say, "Lord if I can't pay rent then I'm going to go back home and go back to my old life." That's how I looked at it, my old life.

I was in LA for nine years before I ended up losing my apartment. I just couldn't afford to pay my rent anymore.

I received a clear message from God saying, "No. Just stay put."

While I was in eviction court fighting unsuccessfully to try and stay in my apartment, I called an industry friend who knew what was going on and asked "Is it ok if I still come stay there?"

She said, "Sure."

Shortly after that, I hit another challenge. My mom passed away. I was so angry. I thought, "Lord. You stripped me of all my money, and now you took my mom too?"

I remember God said, "This is an opportunity to pray." So, I prayed and prayed. God quickly granted me peace.

Looking back, I know that the whole situation was in God's hand. He was preparing me to move to another level in my life.

THE LESSON OF FAITH

"Trust in the Lord with all your heart and lean not on your own understanding; in all your ways submit to Him, and He will make your paths straight." Proverbs 3:5-6 (NIV)

Trust. I learned to trust. I learned to trust what I hear from God.

That has been an issue with me because I'm used to living my life the way I see fit instead of according to the instruction of the Holy Spirit. I have to trust God with everything from what I eat, to the clothes that I wear.

INTO ABUNDANCE

Blu Skin Care, LLC is a company that God himself started. I didn't want to start a skin care line.

I thought, "I'm an actress. It makes more sense for me to do television shows and films."

I'd lie in bed and hear God say over and over, "Start a skin care line." I'm like, "Oh yeah? With what money, God?"

I started to think I was crazy. I called a few trusted friends and confessed, "I believe I'm hearing God tell me to start a skin care line. Pray that I'm actually hearing from Him."

What it's taught me for my business is to listen to Him no matter how crazy it may sound. Of course, I've gone through craziness, so I clearly know the difference.

No matter what it looks like, no matter what I may think, I just need to trust what He's telling me to do. I must take out what I want to happen or what I think should happen or shouldn't happen. I just trust. He has guided me all the way.

APPLICATION

The first thing is to allow God to train you to hear from Him in your business operations, the studying of scriptures, having accountability partners, and in prayer.

You also have to start off with worship. Worship Him to get your body and mind in a place where you can hear from Him. Thinking back on the things He took me through, had I not worshipped Him, I would have never been strong enough to follow His leading.

PRAYER

"Oh Heavenly Father, who has filled the whole earth with beauty. Open my eyes to clearly see Your gracious hand in all Your works. Strengthen me to continue serving You with gladness and thanksgiving. Give me a clean heart. It's because of Your precious Son, Jesus Christ who died on the cross for my sins that I'm not given what I deserve, which is eternal damnation. It is in the precious name of the one who was once dead but is now alive interceding on my behalf that I pray. Thank you Father for your grace and mercy.

DAILY DECLARATION

Stop waiting on someone to help you. Help someone waiting on you. #FaithIntoAbundance

MEET ZONDRA WILSON

After booking numerous modeling jobs for billion-dollar companies such as Merz, Best Buy, and Pfizer, Zondra Wilson decided to launch a USDA certified organic skin care line. Blu Skin Care, LLC manufacturers the only American-made USDA certified organic

powdered facial cleanser sold in the United States. Zondra is also the only female, African American owner, manufacturer and distributor of a skin care company with USDA certified organic accreditation in the United States.

So, why the name "Blu Skin Care?" In the Bible, the color blue is sometimes associated with the commandments of God, the importance of remembering them and also the heavenly calling of those who had been chosen by God to be His people (Numbers 15:38-40). Therefore, "Blu Skin Care" was the obvious name for the company.

"Blu" prides itself on sourcing the purest and most potent ingredients including organic in all of its formulations.

Cruelty Free, Gluten Free, Non-GMO, Vegan, No Parabens, No Polymers, No Sulphates, No Artificial Colors or Fragrances

Our ingredients are plant-derived and formulated with botanicals. We are committed to all of our products being non-GMO as well as nutritious for your skin and as close to 100% USDA certified organic whenever possible.

We promise to support a comprehensive approach to educating people on how to eat right, not only for good health but also for fantastic skin. We encourage you to enjoy a diverse, plant-based diet that provides a full range of nutrients. "Blu Skin Care, LLC" relies on foods known to promote health and support recovery from illness and injury. It integrates the very best of both ancient and modern nutritional approaches to form a flexible system of wholeness. At "Blu", we serve the organic skin care industry with the passion and depth of experience that can only come with a lifetime of commitment to the organic movement. We service customers with all skin types.

CONTACT ZONDRA

Blu Skin Care, LLC

WEBSITE
BluSkinCare.info

FACEBOOK
Facebook.com/BluSkinCare

INSTAGRAM
@bluskincare

TWITTER
@bluskincare

DAY 29

THE PASSENGER
THAT WASN'T THERE

DON SCHNURE

"Have I not commanded you? Be strong and courageous. Do not be frightened, and do not be dismayed, for the Lord your God is with you wherever you go."

Joshua 1:9

It was the fall of 1985. I was friends with a circle of people who were all younger than me. Because they were starting school and beginning new careers, they didn't have a lot of time to keep in contact. We didn't have social media or texting back then, so the lines of communication were limited.

I went out and tried to meet new people, but it was difficult. I felt as if I had a big hole in my heart. I felt empty. It was then that I realized I was, in a sense, using my friends as a source of validation.

One night, I went out on a date with a woman I had met. We had a wonderful time and I took her home at about 11:30 p.m. After I had dropped her off, I hit the highway to go home. Suddenly, I got an overwhelming sense that someone was sitting adjacent to me in the passenger seat.

I looked over saw nothing, but I could still feel a presence with me inside the car. It may sound ridiculous, but I felt that presence put its hand on my shoulder. It was a feeling of reassurance that everything was going to be okay.

Over the next few weeks, that same ominous occurrence happened about three or four more times. I have no explanation why, but it made me feel better.

THE LESSON OF FAITH

What I learned was that I'm not the center of the universe. I am a part of something that I was not even aware I was part of before. I came to realize that I had to look outside of myself for answers to my questions, and that is what led me to accept God as my savior.

Seeking Christ saved me from falling into a depression, which could have potentially caused me to be emotionally, mentally, and spiritually lost for who knows how long. Unlike a lot of some believers, I was not introduced to Jesus Christ by another believer. It was that spiritual, reassuring presence that caused me to realize that I needed to let go of my desire to run my life and let God run it instead.

INTO ABUNDANCE

The way I've been able to apply this lesson to my business is that I apply it to my life. I realize that my business is part of my life.

I know a lot of business associates who, in my opinion, have it backwards. Their business is their life. That dictates everything to them and ultimately, no matter what sort of financial success they have, not one of them is happy. They work too much, they miss their kids, they're in bad health, they're overweight, or they can't sleep.

I realized that even though I'm the sole proprietor and I run my own company, I'm not by myself. I realized that there has to be a balance.

APPLICATION

I think it's a matter of making sure that your priorities are in alignment with your value system. Making sure that you do not get caught up in the worldly attainment of things at the expense what's really important.

You need to stop and ask God for help. *What am I not doing right that I need to do?* Then just wait.

Patience is probably the most underrated, but valuable trait for an entrepreneur. We can get that only through prayer.

PRAYER

We need you, Lord. I need you. I need you to wrap your arms around me and help me understand that it's a good thing I don't understand everything. You are God. And I am not. May I anticipate the exquisite work of Your hands to transform my nothing into Your everything.

DAILY DECLARATION

Patience is probably the most underrated, but valuable trait for an entrepreneur, and you can only get it through prayer. #FaithIntoAbundance.

MEET DON SCOTT SCHNURE

Don Scott Schnure is a digital marketing professional, software designer and video producer since 1997. He's built and sold software in dozens of markets, including SEO, Media Publishing, Email Marketing, Internet safety and monitoring for kids, and of course online e-commerce solutions.

As the founder of 1AutomationWiz.com, the original all in one e-commerce solution, Don helps new and existing business owners simplify the complex task of both selling and marketing their products online.

His specialties include: E-commerce, Search Engine Optimization, Internet Marketing Strategies, Personal Persuasion, Direct Marketing, Video Production, Copywriting, Facebook Organic Reach Strategies.

CONTACT DON

1AutomationWiz.com

WEBSITE
1AutomationWiz.com

FACEBOOK
Facebook.com/DonSchnure

INSTAGRAM
@donschnure

TWITTER
@DonSchnure

LINKEDIN
LinkedIn.com/in/DonSchnure

THE CRAVING

HOWARD PARTRIDGE

> *"I have the right to do anything," you say—but not everything is beneficial.*
>
> *"I have the right to do anything"—but I will not be mastered by anything.*
>
> *1 Corinthians 6:12*

I grew up going to a Baptist church and was baptized at nine years old, but I didn't know Christ. When I turned fifteen, I became a rebellious teenager, and I stopped going to church.

Fast forward twelve years to 1987, I was 27 years old and still had the terrible marijuana habit that I began when I was fifteen. For twelve years, this habit gripped me. I'd been in business for three years, but all I could think about was getting high every day.

Suddenly, a strange thing happened to me. I got this sort of overwhelming feeling that came out of nowhere. It was just this sense that I needed to change, and somehow, strangely, I knew that I needed to give my life to Jesus.

I don't know how I knew that. At the time, I had three employees, and they were all having the same feeling. The feeling got stronger and stronger and stronger, and it was almost like a warning. It was as if God had reached down and grabbed ahold of my heart and just wouldn't let it go.

As soon as I made the decision to give my life to Jesus, I came to this place where felt like there was really nothing else to live for.

I decided to give my life to Jesus and became a Christian right then and there.

The first miracle was that I got my mind back, and I was delivered from my marijuana addiction instantly. It's been almost thirty years, and I have never ever had another inkling for it. The craving was just gone.

I know people who have struggled with addictions all their life. I was very grateful that I was able to beat my addiction and my whole life changed. All three of my employees became great Christian men as well. I was put on a new path, and life has been incredible since.

THE LESSON OF FAITH

God wanted me in His kingdom. God wanted to use me. He cared enough about me that He called me. I think that that's the lesson that everybody else can take away: He wants you, He loves you, He created you.

He wants a relationship with you.

INTO ABUNDANCE

I have led associates, partners, employees, customers, and neighbors to the Lord. It's just amazing. At our conference, we have a spiritual night and people have been set free and saved there.

Recently, I was talking to a colleague of mine about his son, who is an adult now, and he said, "Man, he's come a long way since that day that you and I prayed in that used car parking lot."

I didn't even remember praying with him that day.

Just the other day, my neighbor came over to me, and he said, "I need to talk to you." He just buried his head in my chest and just bawled like a baby, and said, "I need God in my life."

APPLICATION

I think that what we need to understand is that we're not living in two different worlds, that it's all one package. Once you come to know the Lord, you are a new creature.

You don't separate it on Sunday.

It's not "act one way at work and act some other way at church." This is not a religion. It's a faith. It changes who you are.

To begin, pray every day, read the Word, trust God, ask God for advice, trust Him through those times, and really care about people, and invest in people.

Pray for others, help them, and build a relationship with them. You don't need to preach to them, just serve them, help them, and let them see your light. This doesn't mean that you don't ever say anything, but you say it at the proper time with the leading of the Lord.

Pray for people, minister to people, and share with them.

PRAYER

Father God, we thank you for all of creation and we thank you for the gift of our Family, Friends and Loved ones in our lives. We thank you that we can be a blessing to them, and that they can in return can be a blessing to us when needed. We thank you for the gift of Jesus Christ, and also for the sacrifice of Jesus for all of our sins. We praise You God, Holy Spirit and Jesus Christ.

DAILY DECLARATION

I am a phenomenal product created to BE phenomenal, to DO phenomenal things and to have a phenomenal life. #FaithIntoAbundance

MEET HOWARD PARTRIDGE

Howard Partridge is an international business coach with coaching members in 97 industries in seven countries. He is a best selling author of four books that reached #1 on Amazon in at least one category, the exclusive business coach for the Zig Ziglar Corporation, the first Ziglar Legacy Trainer in the world, the first founding member of The John Maxwell Team, and a DISC Certified Human Behavior Expert.

Howard grew up on welfare in Mobile Alabama and left home at age 18. He arrived in Houston, Texas on a Greyhound bus with only 25 cents in his pocket. He started his first business out of the trunk of his car over 30 years ago and built it into a multi-million dollar enterprise. He has owned nine small businesses altogether and owns four companies at the time of this printing.

He is president of Phenomenal Products, Inc. which helps small business owners stop being a slave to their business by transforming it into a predictable, profitable, turnkey operation. For the past two decades, Howard has helped small business owners around the world dramatically improve their businesses.

He has led hundreds of seminars, webinars, workshops and holds his own live multi-day events which have featured some of America's top business trainers including John Maxwell, Michael Gerber, Bob Burg, Dr. Joseph A. Michelli, Darren Hardy, Dr. Robert Rohm and American legend Zig Ziglar.

Howard is married to Denise and has one beautiful son, Christian.

CONTACT HOWARD

Phenomenal Products, Inc.

WEBSITE
HowardPartridge.com

FACEBOOK
Facebook.com/HowardPartridgePPI

INSTAGRAM
@HowardPartridge

TWITTER
@HowardPartridge

LINKEDIN
LinkedIn.com/in/Howard-Partridge-6920b83

DAY 31

NO FOOD TO EAT

MAYRA FERNANDEZ

> *"But if anyone has the world's goods and sees his brother in need, yet closes his heart against him, how does God's love abide in him?*
>
> *Little children, let us not love in word or talk, but in deed and in truth."*
>
> *1 John 3:17-18*

In life, we learn innumerable lessons, some of which have larger effects on us than others. The most impactful lesson I have learned in life comes from my childhood.

I was raised by my mother, who independently raised three children. She was a very strong woman and a faithful believer. Although my mother worked hard to provide for my siblings and me, we faced many hardships.

There were times when we had no food to eat. Our clothes grew worn and used because we could not afford new ones. I had a ruffled light blue shirt that I wore almost every day. We often bounced from apartment to apartment while my mother struggled to make ends meet.

I remember that during most of my elementary school years, at school would be the only time I would eat a good meal – breakfast and lunch.

I'd wake up ready for school not only because I enjoyed the learning and the play time, but most of all the warm oatmeal I would get to eat. After not eating since lunch the previous day, it tasted heavenly every single morning.

I don't remember ever asking my mother for more than she could give. I was a happy content child. I'll always remember those moments and count my blessings as they remind me how blessed I have been.

Nevertheless, my mother would always make sure to say to us, "Don't give up. We are going to get through this," and we always did. My mother's unwavering example of faith and knowing that we always did get through those tough times eventually caused me to covet a stronger faith and belief in the Lord.

THE LESSON OF FAITH

My often troublesome childhood in conjunction with my mother's unfaltering faith in the midst of dark times has taught me many lessons, most notably the lesson that perseverance is key in the face of adversity.

There is a bible scripture that tells us God does not give us more than we can handle, and that He will stand by us throughout our troubled times. I deeply believe that.

INTO ABUNDANCE

I own and operate a modest preschool learning center, which has enabled me to interact with numerous children and families.

I have experienced several ups and downs throughout the journey that is starting and maintaining a small business. Many times the ups overshadowed the downs.

There were points at which my business was on its proverbial deathbed, and worrisome thoughts like "How am I going to get through this?" ran rampant in my mind. It was at times like these that I would be reminded of both my mother's faith and endurance in the midst of difficult times as well as the power of prayer.

Prayer and faith in God are simultaneously the most powerful tools for success as well as my greatest weapons against adversity.

APPLICATION

I want you to apply this lesson to your life in the same way that I have. We must be able to accept the inevitable presence of obstacles in life without letting those obstacles intimidate us.

We experience, read about, and hear about hardship every single day, and it is natural for us to ask, "God where are you? Why is this world so lost?"

It is at these times we must remember that God is always present and working in and on our lives.

PRAYER

2 Corinthians 4:16-18 Therefore we do not lose heart. Though outwardly we are wasting away, yet inwardly we are being renewed day by day. For our light and momentary troubles are achieving for us an eternal glory that far outweighs them all. So we fix our eyes not on what is seen, but on what is unseen. For what is seen is temporary, but what is unseen is eternal.

DAILY DECLARATION

Stay Focused, Stay Determined and in all things give Praise and Glory to the one above. #FaithIntoAbundance

MEET MAYRA FERNANDEZ

Mayra Fernandez is an entrepreneur who owns and operates a small business that focuses on early childhood education and the development stages of young children from infancy to five years old.

Mayra has been in business for over 14 years, has a Masters degree in Early Childhood Development and Education from the University of Houston – Clearlake, and graduated in the top of her class. She received her Bachelor of Science in Business Administration from Trinity University. Mayra is also a member of several early childhood organizations in which Directors like herself gather and discuss ongoing topics in the industry.

Mayra's early childhood center is one of several centers chosen by the Texas Department of Family and Protective Services as a training site for their newly hired inspectors. She is currently working on expanding her business into a bigger commercial location. She has also been involved with Collaborative for Children, a non-profit dedicated to building a strong educational foundation for young children to succeed in school and life.

In her free time, she enjoys traveling and exploring new cultures, reading, dancing, concerts, and the arts. She lives an active lifestyle in which she runs, bikes, and swims as a triathlete. Mayra completed her very first full Ironman in May of 2016.

CONTACT MAYRA

LINKEDIN
LinkedIn.com/in/Mayra-Fernandez-6782a628

FACEBOOK
Facebook.com/Mayra.Fernandez.779

INSTAGRAM
@mayrafern

DAY 32

JOY IS SERIOUS BUSINESS

LORY MOORE

> *Do not grow weary in doing good, for at just the right time we will reap a harvest of blessing, if we don't give up. So, whenever we have the opportunity, we should do good to everyone—especially to those in the family of faith.*
>
> *Galatians 6:9-10*

"Man, I love your smile!" "I don't know how you are always so happy!" After half a century on the planet, as George Orwell famously observed, I do believe that we have the "face that we deserve." I am grateful that my smile–that crooked, wrinkles-increasing-on-the-edges slice of my soul–is the single feature that almost everyone remembers most about me.

What might not be so evident to someone unfamiliar with my life experience is that the positive attitude I reflect is not some happy-go-lucky, superficial, smiley-face emoji. Behind the smile, I've experienced deep sorrow, such as being a comfort to my aunt, my best friend, my business mentor, and my business partner's four-year-old daughter as each of them went to Jesus after battling cancer, all during a four month time frame. Or the gut-wrenching moment when I was on a beach in Hawaii with my five-year-old son and I got the cellphone call with the news that my two-year-old niece had been diagnosed with a vicious form of childhood cancer, and rushed back home to be with my brother and his family as they fought the demon head-on. Or the mind-numbing feeling of walking my four children through the sudden deaths of their fathers, not once but twice, praying for the strength and wisdom to explain the unexplainable, as I help each of them struggle to deal with a level of anguish and bewilderment no child should have to bear.

These excruciatingly painful, heart-wrenching moments brought me to my knees, and if it wasn't for my faith I would have stayed there in a crumpled heap. When tragedy strikes, it is so easy to get overwhelmed in the stifling sorrow of the moment. Because no matter what our best-laid plans are, life often seems to follow a script with much more pain and hardship than we would ever write for ourselves. Through a life-long series of gut punches and right hooks, I've had to learn how to not only pull myself off the ground, feeling bloodied, battered and bruised, but also to turn around and give a hand up to those I love who've been knocked down and out themselves.

It's not that the tears stop flowing. No. It's that with the assurance of Christ, I can face the struggle and pain through the tears. I can help a family crushed with the reality of their pint-sized superhero battling a life-threatening disease, by bringing casseroles or playing Nerf-tag with their other children to bring some much-needed normalcy to their lives. Or help the parents visualize the powerful image of that pre-school baby growing into a strong-willed teenager with rainbow painted fingers and toes (and attitude for days), victorious over the cancer dragon that seems so unconquerable in the current moment.

And when the path seems steeper and rockier than I could possibly bear, when someone I love beyond my own life loses theirs, I have to muster the best in me that I have to give. Over and over, I remind myself that, during and after the crushing pain of loss, I can celebrate and honor the lives of my loved ones by nurturing, focusing and shining the light of their lives that remains inside of me. Organize a fundraiser to end a killer disease, or show up with overflowing baskets of fluffy, stuffed animals to bring a smile to the faces of little ones battling on. Light a candle to remember and honor a beautiful life. Help my children reflect on and enhance the 50% of themselves that is their Dad, and dedicate the best in them to him, in their daily walk and in the impact of their own lives.

Just showing up and living life with joy, in ways big and small, no matter how messy the journey becomes. As C.S. Lewis beautifully phrased it, "Joy is the serious business of Heaven." All because, and only because, by faith, we know we are on the winning team.

THE LESSON OF FAITH

Beyond happiness, through all the ups and downs of my life it was the joy of the Lord that was my strength, the knowledge that God is faithful, and no matter what life throws at me, I can claim victory and joy today. Rejoicing doesn't mean an absence of sorrow; it is the blessed assurance that God is in control. Over every. Single. Thing.

Even now as I write the final edit on my chapter of this book, I am typing from a hospital room in ICU, where my mother is hooked up to a breathing machine and seemingly miles of tubes and needles, feeling helpless as I pray for the most capable hands to guide her through this medical emergency that, try as I might, I don't have the capacity to change. Even though I could muster the supernatural strength to lift her into the car and out into a wheelchair when we arrived after our frantic drive to the ER two days ago, my love and adrenaline can't fix the inside issues that are threatening her life.

But I know who does have the power. I don't have to rely on my own strength, because I wasn't promised a life with no trouble. I've got something better: the promise that through ANY trouble, I don't have to fear because Christ is stronger than anything the world has the audacity to throw at me. Even typing in a stiff, cold chair with emergency medical equipment beeping and buzzing all around me, I am rejoicing and grateful for the moment. Even more so when the puzzled ICU nurse says to me, "I don't know what it is, but I want some of what you have that keeps you so full of joy." As a Christian, I am equipped to "flip the script" to place a Jesus filter over all life experiences. All with the assurance that God and I, and my precious, God-fearing Momma and Daddy, my children and family and all others who follow Christ, win in the end.

INTO ABUNDANCE

The single greatest predictor of success for an entrepreneur is their resilience, their ability to get knocked down, rise up and start again, in business and in life. A successful entrepreneur understands that failure isn't the end of the story; it's just another chapter in the book. Failure is opportunity in disguise; a learning experience to move your business down the path to success, provided you never give up.

As a Christian entrepreneur, we have an extra layer that allows us not just to survive but thrive, to literally and figuratively jump up with joy no matter what setbacks or cutbacks get in our way. Once you have your eyes firmly set on your "why", that burning-in-the-belly "this is why I'm meant to be here" core purpose for being, you understand that Joy is YOUR serious business. When you are fulfilling your God-given destiny, regardless of the product or service you sell, when you are reflecting Christ and having an impact in the world, God has you covered. When you fall down, He will pick you up. When you stumble again and again and yet again, He will be there.

Making a profit is a necessary goal in business, but where you flip the script as a Christian entrepreneur is the moment you make the decision to serve God with your business. In that exact moment, you have stepped into the abundant life--before one penny hits your bank account. Your abundance is not dependent on a dollar sign. As long as you are in a place of service and giving, you ARE living an abundant life. Even if the world calls you a fool when you choose "Return on Impact" over "Return on Investment", you can dance with joy knowing that your treasure chest is overflowing, now and into eternity.

DAILY DECLARATION

I will be fearless, faithful and focused on using my gifts and talents to bless others in the highest and best way, so that their lives and mine may be changed for good. #FaithIntoAbundance

PRAYER

Holy Father, Today as I face this new day that You have made, please grant me self control to seek to understand others first; gentleness to turn a potential conflict into a blessing for someone in my world, and faithfulness to follow your calling even when life turns out other than my well-laid plans. I pray to sow Goodness in every interaction, despite the knowledge that I may never see them sprout or grow in my lifetime, Kindness to lighten a stranger's load when they most need a helping hand, and Patience to listen to harsh words spoken by a hurting soul, for whom I may be the only ears to listen today. I pray for Peace to rest in each moment as a perfect gift from you, even when the wrapping is unfamiliar or uncomfortable; I pray that I will find Joy, through you, in ALL things, especially the ones where the joy is so hidden as to be unrecognizable to human eyes, so that others may see my reaction and be filled with longing for whatever it is in me that brings such delight. And, most deeply of all, I pray that I may reflect Love, your unconditional, all-consuming love, to each and every person that you divinely place in my path today, that their lives can be changed, for good, by even what little I do.

MEET LORY MOORE

Dr. Lory Moore is an attorney, author, speaker, successful entrepreneur and passionate marketing consultant who currently is a proud citizen of Fort Worth, Texas. Lory's life's passion is training the people she calls "the new heroes" (entrepreneurs) to make an impact in the world by showing them how to generate profits from their strengths, and how to multiply their impact by sowing those seeds back into society. From former corporate executives repurposing their lives into encore entrepreneurial careers, to

Millennials eager to find their way in creative social enterprises, to non-profit staff and board members learning to capitalize on diverse residual income streams, Lory loves to educate and guide others to fulfill their purpose, while making a meaningful living.

An award-winning advocate and former judge, her latest project is creating, coordinating and co-teaching a college curriculum on Social Entrepreneurship. Together with brilliant, bold and business-savvy leaders, she is thrilled to be part of a movement that is showing how giving -- bringing purpose to profits -- is the surest path to business success.

Lory enjoys mentoring her five children, three grandchildren and other youth in leadership development and various athletic competitions during her spare time. In fact, it's those fascinating youth who keep her on the cutting edge of social media and emerging technology that can help her clients gain the competitive advantage in an ever-changing economy. As she is known for saying in her business trainings, "If you need help deciphering your technology…hand it to your three year old!"

CONTACT LORY

Partnering With Purpose, LLC

WEBSITES
LoryMoore.com
PartneringWithPurpose.com

FACEBOOK
Facebook.com/Lory.Moore1

LINKEDIN
LinkedIn.com/in/LoryMoore

TWITTER
@lorymoore

Made in the USA
Charleston, SC
12 January 2017